ADVANCE REVIEWS

"Starting right out of the gate with his clever, catchy and concise tease, in *My Scripted and Unscripted Life* Tony Pagnotti delivers an insightful, heartfelt, and human account of his journey to, in front of, and behind the camera. His compelling account of the news business from his perspective will pull you from page to page."

> —Steve Geppi, Publisher, *Baltimore Magazine*,
> Gemstone Publishing

"Reporter Pagnotti provides a valuable road map for future journalists with his captivating experiences on the colorful front lines of TV news."

> — Al Primo, Creator/Developer of TV EYEWITNESS NEWS

"Always the gentleman, Tony had a knack for excelling as a standup versatile reporter who could do it all from spot news to the weather!"

> — Dr. Frank Field, iconic NBC & CBS New York meteorologist and author

My Scripted and Unscripted Life

A Memoir of a TV Newsman

My Scripted and Unscripted Life

A Memoir of a TV Newsman

TONY PAGNOTTI

Apprentice
House Press
Loyola University Maryland

First Edition

Hardcover ISBN: 978-1-62720-341-8
Paperback ISBN: 978-1-62720-342-5
Ebook ISBN: 978-1-62720-343-2

Printed in the United States of America

Acquisitions & Editing: Annabelle Finagin
Design: Apprentice House Press
Promotion plan: Tyler Zorn
Managing editor: Kelley Chan

Published by Apprentice House Press

Apprentice
House Press
Loyola University Maryland

Apprentice House Press
Loyola University Maryland
4501 N. Charles Street
Baltimore, MD 21210
410.617.5265
www.ApprenticeHouse.com
info@ApprenticeHouse.com

Dedicated to the Ones I Love

To Alee and Annie who growing up were taught that Must See TV meant to always watch their Dad on Television.

And to my biggest fan, my late mother. When I graduated from college she wrote a personal letter to CBS iconic anchorman asking him to please get her son a job.

INTRODUCTION

What you're about to read wasn't originally intended to be a book. It was a required graduate thesis for a degree in Contemporary Communications that I was pursuing at the College of Notre Dame, Maryland in 2010. After 25 years as a TV Newsman at various stations around the country, I decided to make a career change. As much as I loved my livelihood, I decided I wanted to pursue another long-time passion: teaching college students the importance of mastering communication skills in order to succeed in any given career. But I discovered that, despite my decades of professional experience, colleges would only hire instructors with a minimum of a Master's Degree.

So, when it came time for me to decide on what extensive scholarly research project I would take on, my advisor – Dr. Gene Farrington, a published novelist himself – suggested, "How about an in-depth look at the business of local television, as seen through the eyes of broadcaster who has been there and done that?"

"But would the College's Review committee consider that proposal scholarly enough to meet Notre Dame's high academic standards required to obtain a Master's Degree?" I asked.

"Why not?", replied the old professor, "provided it's written with eloquence, introspection and insight."

As I began my writing, I soon realized that this manuscript would take on somewhat of an autobiographical tone. I couldn't talk about my livelihood without detailing my life, with all its ups and downs and some of the people who were there along the way.

From my college days at Boston University, followed by the many rungs I had taken in both climbing and descending the TV ladder, you'll discover how celebrities such as Howard Stern, Bill O'Reilly and Al Roker are connected to my colorful career. There are other names in the book that I have changed to perhaps avoid any hard feelings from colleagues who might not enjoy my candid comments.

QUIET ON THE SET and CUE TALENT.

Tony Pagnotti
May 2020

1

THE BIRTH OF A BROADCASTER

Close Up: Tony on camera
THANKS FOR JOINING US ON
WPAG-TV NEWS. COMING UP:
I'LL LET YOU KNOW WHY MY UNCLE
HAD TO DIE IN ORDER FOR
ME TO BREAK INTO BROADCASTING

How about that for making sure you won't put this book down for at least the next few pages? Clever, Catchy and Concise tease, huh? I learned the importance of following the 3 C's of broadcast writing during my first job in television: WLOS in Asheville, North Carolina. Fresh out of Boston University in 1976, I was hired by the station's News Director who, on the first day of the job, told me,

"Forget all the crap they taught you in college, kid. If you want to make it big in this business someday, you've got to write the way people talk. The key are the 3 C's. And it all begins with you being able to keep them watching for the entire hour – that's what boosts the ratings. The better the ratings, the higher the cost for the commercials our sales department charges the advertisers. That's what ensures we get our paychecks once a week."

The secret, he snickered, to luring viewers into watching the news is the "Hey, Martha" story. I sheepishly confessed that my college professors never mentioned Martha during my broadcast journalism classes. He shot back, "When Joe Six-Pack sits down to watch the news and he hears a great 3 C tease, he yells into the other room, 'Hey, Martha, you have to come in here and see this story is coming up on the news.'"

When Martha or Marty watch the local TV news, they are invited by the friendly anchor folks to sit and wait and not turn the channel until they get the rest of the story. There could be some tease like, "You might hold off on having that second cup of coffee, until you see our story coming up on the adverse effects of caffeine consumption." After patiently sitting through weather and sports reports they have little interest in, the viewers resist the urge not to go to the kitchen for a java refill during all the commercials. Then comes the story they've been waiting for:

A Medical research team in Oslo has found that increased caffeine consumption on a daily basis can cause hyperactivity and overt agitation. The scientists conducted a survey with laboratory rats over a period of six months and found that the rodents who were injected with twice the amount of 100% roast Columbian coffee than the other mice became physically abusive to their less-caffeinated test participants. So, perhaps we might all consider decaf the next time we go for a refill.

That fifteen-second, much-anticipated story you waited 45 minutes for wasn't exactly chocked-full of new information that will convince you to say, "so long," to Joe forever. But that's okay – it was time well-spent, watching those likeable men and women you welcome into your living rooms every day.

But who are we, anyway? We, the people, who viewers see on a more regular basis than some best friends? We are the ones who make a living on the news at 765 local stations around the country – from the smallest market #209 Glendive Montana, serving just 3,500 households, on up to #1 New York City with a viewership of roughly seven million people. The salary spread is just as huge, with anchors in small markets taking home about $13,000 per year, peanuts in comparison to the annual major market paycheck of a few million dollars.

As wide in range as there is income and professional experience, so is the diversity in our backgrounds and off-air personalities. In the ten TV stations at which I have worked, there are quite a few whom I have admired. Others I have either liked or accepted. And, frankly, in the past 34 years there were only a couple of news bosses whom I have disliked. But don't let me get ahead of myself. The one thing TV news people have in common is our desire to be seen and liked by as many people as possible, without ever letting the viewers get to know the person that they think we really are. What type of individual is attracted to working in a cutthroat industry, where landing a first-time, on-air job is as likely as hitting the lottery? Especially when the initial payoff is not much higher than the annual salary of a grocery store cashier. There is a lot more job security in saying "Paper or plastic?" than there is in "Good Evening, Everyone, coming up tonight..."

In January 1976, I hit the lottery when I got a call from WLOS-TV, located in the scenic heart of the Blue Ridge Mountains (LOS=Land Of Sky). Following my graduation from Boston University, I had begun sending out resume tapes. These I had recorded during my internship at a TV station in my hometown of Scranton, in compensation for my unpaid services of ripping wire copy and doing lunch runs for the newsroom staff. But there was no price to be put on the opportunity it gave me to rub elbows with the newscasters – the same ones I had looked up to as a teen-ager with the hopes of one day following in their footsteps. The first few days of my internship, I had to catch myself from staring at the longtime anchorman and weatherman eating their lunch and telling off-color jokes in the newsroom. A human side of news casting had been revealed to me, of what had before been mere electronic images on my boyhood TV.

But it wasn't one of the seasoned Newswatch 16 veterans that eventually became my mentor. It was a reporter from Long Island, who had only been at the station for about a year in what was his first television job. In that short time, he'd quickly earned a reputation as a no-nonsense journalist by doing confrontational news stories about an alleged "well-connected" Mafioso-affiliated businesses in the area. Viewers tuned in and watched in fascination each night to see the camera rolling, a reporter chasing down well-known big wigs of questionable repute and then asking, "Are you laundering money? Does your company do business with the mob?"

His forceful and abrasive personality often carried over into the newsroom. Walking though the station with a definite swagger, he would ask his colleagues, "Hey, did you see that piece I did last night? That's what more of you reporters and anchors should be doing. The egotistical, tough-talking New Yorker had a soft spot beneath that hardened exterior, one that prompted Bill O'Reiily to take me, a lowly intern, under his wing.

Yes, that Bill O'Reilly who years later went on to be the in-your-face, no nonsense Fox Network commentator. The nightly *No Spin* Zone had the highest prime time ratings of any cable news program.

Back during the Channel 16 days, reporters and anchors would ask me how I could be friends with him. Somehow, I was able to see eye-to-eye with Bill— beyond the fact that we're both six feet five inches tall, of course. Granted, his occasional tirades and the way he talked to people would never get him voted Mr. Congeniality, but I respected him for his excellent writing skills and the compelling style he used in telling each of his stories. One day in the newsroom I shared that compliment with him. From that day on, he went out of his way to edit my writing and even allow me to go out on news stories with him and his photographer. Within a short period of time, he had taught me how to produce impactful reports.

One day, he remarked that Scranton was certainly no New York when it came to its night life. I said, "You just have to know the right places to go." I invited him to hang out at a popular local club, and he took me up on that offer. I wish cell phone cameras had been invented back then so I could have taken a picture of "Disco Bill" out on the dance floor. On our way out of the club, the usually dour O'Reilly was smiling and said he had a good time. As we headed to our cars, he cautioned, "One thing Pagnotti: no need to tell the troops tomorrow what I was up to tonight."

In the final days of my summer internship at Channel 16, Bill told me he would make arrangements with the studio crew for me to record an audition tape I could send out to stations after graduation. Channel 16 management let me go into the studio and practice reading five minutes of copy. After rehearsing several times with the news copy I had written, Bill let me use some of his pancake makeup to conceal beard shadows from the bright studio light. A tape rolled and I delivered my mock newscast with as much energy and sincerity as if it were the real thing. The tape operator handed me what would now be my official resume reel to send out to all those stations I knew were just dying to give me my first job as a TV journalist. Bill told me it wasn't a bad job for a beginner. I was thrilled because in O'Reilly speak that meant I did a great job.

Knowing not to shoot too high, I only answered the ads in *Broadcasting Magazine* that read: *Will consider highly-trainable Broadcast Journalism grads with limited experience who possess on-air potential.* Translation: how cheap are you willing to work, kid? During the course of three months, I sent out several tapes and letters to various stations, only to get enough rejection letters to wallpaper the bedroom in my parent's house where I was living.

Then, on January 15, 1976, it happened. I hit the lottery when my father said, "There's a guy on the phone looking to hire you from Nashville." Couldn't be. The Music City Market #29 was out of my league. It turned out that the caller was actually news director Walt Adams from Asheville, NC. In a very friendly and excitable voice, he told me he had just viewed my tape which, he said, was "a bit green but showed potential."

"Great," I replied. "I'd love to come for an interview, at your convenience."

"Don't need to, kid. I've been in this business for so long, I know budding talent when I see it. You have a very likeable on-air persona. I want to offer you a reporter's position."

Talk about being shocked. I couldn't think of anything to say.

"Hello, Tony, are you there? We must have a bad connection"

"Yes, sir. When would you need me to start?"

"How about two weeks?"

"Sure."

"I want you to know that it's a full-time position, $160 a week with benefits and pay. If that's agreeable to you, I'll have my secretary call tomorrow so she can go over all the paperwork and arrangements."

"Sounds great, Mr. Adams. Thank you for the opportunity. I look forward to meeting you soon."

"Oh, good, and call me Walt.

"Congratulations, kid. I'm going to go tell our news team. A good-looking Italian kid from up North will be a nice addition to the staff."

With a glazed look, I told my mother and father the news. Before any words of congratulations, my father, who had just finished paying off a pretty hefty tuition bill at BU, asked, "So, what will you be making?"

"A hundred and sixty bucks a week."

"You've got to be kidding. That's four dollars an hour... not much more than minimum wage."

"But, dad, only one out of seven hundred broadcast journalism majors winds up getting an on-air job in TV."

He replied "Well, what do the other six hundred and ninety-nine end up doing?"

"Give up and go into other lines of work."

Shrugging his shoulders, he replied "Maybe you should have considered that option before accepting that measly salary from North Carolina."

Ever since I was in grade school, my father's plan was for me to become a pharmacist and take over the successful neighborhood pharmacy that he had built from the ground up. He always regretted that I didn't go to pharmacy school, despite my bad chemistry grades in high school and overall disinterest in becoming a druggist.

"You know it's still not too late for you to apply to pharmacy school, instead of working for peanuts as a broadcaster...."

Right then my mother chimed in, just in time to break the tense dialogue. "We should be proud that we'll have a famous television celebrity in our family."

Go South young man.

2

CAROLINA, HERE I COME

Since the soon-to-be-TV-celebrity didn't have his own car yet, my sister Ann Marie and her boyfriend agreed to drive me the twelve hours south to my new workplace. My first sight as we approached Asheville was the beautiful backdrop of the Smoky Mountains which had me thinking about how exciting living and working here would be. But before I could get too excited, I knew I would need to find an apartment within walking distance from the TV station. That is, until I could afford to buy a car with the checks I'd be getting from what was the career equivalent of hitting the lottery. In the newspaper classifieds I found what was termed a "garage apartment." It was a log exterior, low-ceiling dwelling that was accessed by climbing a few steps up from the three car garage. Not exactly the lap of luxury, but the rent was right: $125.00 per month. That was thirty-five dollars less than one week of my take-home pay.

The next morning, I was feeling extremely nervous on my half mile walk to work, thinking that, by the end of the day, I would probably have made my first TV appearance. What if my writing wasn't up to professional standards? What if I began stuttering, stumbling, or, worse yet, no words came out when I was on camera out on location? I feared that I might be fired on day one and would shamefully have to join the ranks of the 699 communication grads rejected by the TV biz.

My insecurities were soon put to rest. Upon entering the station, I was warmly greeted with a firm handshake by a pint-sized, very animated, red-haired man wearing an ear-to-ear smile.

"Hi. I'm Walt, Tony. Welcome aboard. Bye the way, you won't have to walk to work after today. I'm going to let you take a news-car home with you each day. But you'll also be taking a news-camera with you and will be on call in case there's any spot news. But, quite honestly, you getting a call in the middle of the night will be rare, since – as you'll find out – this isn't exactly Gotham City."

Wow, I thought, *it's like I got a loaner car as part of winning the lottery*. After exchanging a few pleasantries, Walt said he was late for a meeting, but was going to introduce me to one of the other three staff reporters I'd be working with. At first, I felt better when I met Mark Billings He appeared to be only a couple of years older than I was and had been working as a reporter at TV-13 for about a year. As Walt stood by listening, Mark explained that two reporters were paired in a news-car and given a film camera. Each reporter was given an assignment that would air on that night's 6 PM news.

Sounded good to me, being able to ride with someone who knew their way around town and also the comfort of having a more experienced colleague to lend a helping hand. Walt wished me good luck and left the newsroom.

Mark was looking at me with a smirk. "So, what made you come here?"

"Well," I replied enthusiastically, "I graduated from BU and was looking for my first TV gig and Walt called, hired me and here I am, ready to go."

Shaking his head, he said, "Big mistake, this place sucks."

I felt like Mark had torn up my lottery ticket before I could cash it in. With a pained expression, I gasped, "What do you mean?"

"Look, WLOS has always been and will continue to be in the bottom of the ratings against the other two stations – which, by the way, have bigger budgets and much better talent. The owner of this dump has a reputation for paying rock-bottom wages to guys like you and me who are desperate to work in TV. I've been sending out resume tapes since shortly after I arrived at this hell hole and I'd advise you to do the same." He kept going, not coming up for air. "Oh, and, let me tell you, being a Wop from up north isn't going to endear you to the folks around here. Most of them are southern hillbillies who don't like my kind either... a liberal Jew, from Washington, D.C."

I didn't respond immediately, as I was wondering if I might still be able to get back the first month's rent that I paid for my garage apartment. And how long would it take my sister to come get me? But I wasn't quite ready yet to rip up my winning lottery ticket. "Well, Mark, I appreciate your insight and advice but I'm looking forward to doing my first story today."

As we headed out of the newsroom, he shrugged his shoulders and said, "Ok, pal, but don't say I didn't warn you."

We first went to Mark's story at the local board of elections building. As I set up the camera to shoot his story, I noticed that his negative spirit and contempt for the locals disappeared as he graciously interviewed them. During his standup, he looked into the camera with a big smile as he concluded, "Remember tomorrow to get out and vote. *Mark Billings, Dateline News, Asheville.*"

When we got back into the news-car, I complimented him on his poise and professionalism. "Of course I was polite, did you expect me to say how I really feel about all these Bible thumpers who are just going to reelect that same dumb, redneck sheriff?"

I must say that Mark followed the creed taught in all college broadcast journalism courses: Thou shalt not allow your personal or political viewpoints to be incorporated into news presentations, which shall always be fair, balanced, and objective. It was my first realization that TV journalists, like the general public, have various opinions on a variety of topics which we can voice only after the little red light goes off.

Now for my first news story. We drove outside the Asheville town limit into rural Carroll County. My assignment would be to talk to a tobacco farmer about the economic impact being felt by growers as a result of the recent decline in tobacco use.

As much as I wanted to take my time putting the story together, Mark reminded me in his less-than-tactful way: "Don't waste time bullshitting with the farmer. Get done ASAP so we can allow enough time for our news film to be processed and edited for the 6 PM news."

After finishing my interview, I told Mark that I wanted to stand out in the tobacco field to deliver my first standup. He pushed the camera button, a little red light went on, and, pointing a finger, he cued me:

> *So, Farmer Smith says he's worried about the adverse effect that decreasing cigarette usage is having on his livelihood. He, along with the other tobacco farmers of Carroll County, are all concerned that their profits will continue to go up in smoke. I'm Tony Pagnotti, Dateline News, Carroll County.*

I felt a surge of pride and accomplishment that I just recorded my first standup.

Mark hit the camera's off button and snarled, "Sure you don't want to do that over and drop the corny line about going up in smoke? It's a cliché and not good writing."

"No, thanks, I'll keep it."

He grumbled something under his breath as we packed up and headed back to the station.

After each reporter's film reel came out of the station processor, we would stand at an editing bench, cut and splice segments from our raw footage and edit it down into a concise 1:30 news piece called a package. There I was, appearing on film in the mini viewfinder, outstanding in my field, delivering my first standup. There was a daily newsroom routine that, after all the editing was done, reporters, the assignment editor and news director would gather in the newsroom to watch our 6 PM broadcast. The producer told me my tobacco report was the lead story. I thought, *"Wow" my first TV story ever and it was the lead.* Yes, Asheville wasn't exactly a hot bed for big news.

"Well, big guy," Walt Adams smiled, "How was your maiden voyage?"

"Great, I think the story turned out pretty good."

"Well, we're about to see." And with that, we looked up at the TV with a panning shot of the next-door studio and theme music playing…

… The announcer said...

COVERING ALL OF WESTERN NORTH CAROLINA THIS IS DATELINE NEWS...
HERE's anchorman Mike Mason…
Good evening. Thanks for joining us...
Tonight there's worry and concern by farmers in North Carolina that the rapid decline in the sale of cigarettes may eventually drive them out of business. Dateline News reporter Tony Pagnotti has more from Carroll County.

With that, it was official. I was TV talent. As everyone in the newsroom watched, I imagined viewers in TV-land focusing on what I had to say. With my standup closing out the report, I felt like I had made it and had to hold back an urge to scream, "YES."

Following my signoff – *Tony Pagnotti, Dateline*

News... Mike Mason with a close-up shot...
reading from the teleprompter... *We want
to welcome the newest member of the Dateline
News team, Tony Pagnotti.*

With that, my seven newsroom colleagues applauded.
I smiled.

Walt Adams said, "Well, you certainly are off to a great
start. And, by the way, I loved that clever close of 'going up
in smoke.'" I turned my head and next to me was Billings
who mumbled, "What does that jackass know? He's a lousy
news director."

Other than Billings, I found most of my co-workers to
be positive, welcoming and with healthier attitudes toward
WLOS. Anchor Mike Mason, who introduced my first
news story, had been at the station for over two years. He
was a friendly, handsome guy, with blond hair and blue
eyes possessing a twinkle that shone through the TV. The
thirty-five-year-old had what television consultants call that
"made-for-TV look," which explains why his winning lottery ticket was practically handed to him. He told me that
after graduating from college as a history major he returned
to his hometown of Fort Wayne, Indiana, to decide if he
would pursue graduate school. In the meantime, he took
a job as salesman at a men's clothing store. One day, a
customer asked if he had ever considered TV as a career.
As it turns out, the customer was the general manager of
the local station, which was looking for a weekend anchor.
Even though Mike said it sounded like a great opportunity,
he didn't know the first thing about being a reporter, let
alone an anchorman.

"No problem, you've got the raw materials," the guy told him. "Leave the rest to us."

Mike said that the next thing he knew, the station sent him to learn the tricks of the trade at *Masters Research/Consulting Inc.*, a very well-known consulting firm based in Texas. With a hefty list of clients around the country, the "TV Doctors," as they are called, instruct stations on everything from the proper interior design to consider when choosing the right look of news studio set to selecting, writing and delivering the news in a carefully prescribed manner. In addition, the company has a TV talent school where stations can send their anchors to be schooled on the fine art of reading a teleprompter to convey just the right feeling or emotion appropriate for a particular story. While I have never been fortunate to receive such tutelage, anchor friends of mine tell me that they sit in a studio in Iowa as a consultant advises them to "search from within" to connect with the appropriate emotion: *Happy, Sad, Reflective, and Inquisitive.* While you may say that this sounds like acting class, *Masters* prefers to call the sessions "Telegenic Techniques 101." For the various consultants who also do this training for affiliate stations, these sessions are important, because they believe that how well an anchor team connects with its viewing public determines how successfully that station will be in scoring high ratings. That might explain why most anchor people earn at least three times as much as the reporters on staff.

Mike said that, after an intense week at broadcasting boot camp, he was hired at WFWI as their weekend anchor man. After honing his skills there for two years and developing quite a following, Mike, hoping to climb up the TV ladder, started sending resume tapes out – including one to WLOS, who was looking for a main 6 PM anchor. Walt Adams flew him into Asheville for an interview. Anchors get wined and dined and courted by management before they are hired, yet another benefit that they have over the lesser-paid, lowly reporters. He accepted the job. Mike said he, his wife and their two young kids loved Asheville but confided that his contract would be up in six months and he was sending out tapes again.

"Frankly, I would like to work here for another three years, but I know management will be willing to pay me half of what I could probably be making now in a larger market." I had heard through the sour grapevine that Mike was pulling down a whopping $33,000 per year, which was three times what this rookie reporter was making. While I still felt fortunate to be among the chosen few working in TV, I thought that, to ensure a brighter and more illustrious future, I should start grooming myself to become an anchorman.

So, when I asked Walt if he would consider me for any anchor fill-in work, he said, "As a matter of fact, our weekend girl Lisa has a day off Saturday and I need somebody to fill in. Think you can handle it, big fella?"

Quicker than you can say, "Good Evening everyone," I answered, "I sure can."

"Ok," said Walt, "Meet up with her today and she'll tell you what you need to do."

Trying to contain my boyish broadcasting excitement, I stopped by Lisa's desk and told her that I would be in the anchor chair on Saturday.

"Great. Here's what your day will look like. First, you'll come in around 8:30 in the morning. Clear the news wires and find a story and two shorter voice-over stories to read in the studio."

"Oh," I asked, "Is there no reporter working that day to do a story?" She shook her head and smiled. "Come on, you've been working here long enough to know that they aren't going to pay a reporter to come in on Saturday or Sunday. As a weekend anchor, you are a one-man band. You'll come back from shooting your stories by noon and write and edit them. Then, you start selecting from the news wires stories that you'll be using and determine how much time to allot for weather and sports."

"You mean there isn't a producer to do that, like during the week?"

She rolled her eyes and continued, "Then, you should spend your afternoon writing all the copies and teases so that you can have your script ready by 5:00 PM. You also have to select the chroma key slides from this drawer for the control room to electronically superimpose over your shoulder. So, for example, if there's a story on the economy, you would use the slide depicting a big green dollar bill. At 5:30 the director will come into the newsroom to review and mark camera shots."

Whew, I thought, *at least there's a director.*

"At about five minutes 'till six, the director will head to the control upstairs and you'll take your seat in the studio.

18

Put on a mike, the opening news music will play and away you go." Lisa concluded.

"Any questions?"

"Ah, not right now. But how about if need some help on Saturday?"

"Well, I'd love to say you can call me, but I'll be out of town at a wedding. And, unless it's an emergency, Walt doesn't like to be bothered at home on the weekend.

"You'll be fine. Break a leg, anchorman."

3

THE MAIDEN VOYAGE –
AN ANCHOR SINKS

Weekends at most TV stations are operated with a skeleton crew, but at Dateline News it was more like bare bones. When I got in at nine on Saturday morning, the Newsroom was more like Ghostline News. Empty. As I began sorting through the AP wire teletype scripts that accumulated into big rolls overnight, I figured someone else would be coming in soon. I didn't have time to wait around and find out, though, since the local wire said that the county sheriff had arrested a man for operating moonshine while still on his property. Welcome to the hills of western North Carolina, folks, where, even in 1976, some law-breaking residents were making and selling moonshine. So, I went to the sheriff's office and interviewed him, along with filming the confiscated fifty gallon still, which reeked so much of alcohol, I was wondering if the fumes I was inhaling would cause me to shoot out-of-focus footage.

When I got back to the station by mid-afternoon, Dateline Newsroom was still a ghost town. I figured sooner or later at least the director had to show up, since anchoring and directing a show at the same time was impossible even for the most seasoned pro. Then, I heard someone walking into the newsroom. *Ah,* I thought, *finally, I'm no longer alone.*

"Hi. You must be the director."

"No, I'm Ron Page, the film processor. Who are you?"

"Oh, I'm Tony Pagnotti; I'm the new reporter. I'll be anchoring tonight, filling in for Lisa."

"Greeeeat Day," Ron replied in a heavy, drawn-out southern drawl. "These managers round here, just kill me. Throwing a rookie reporter into the hot seat. Oh, well, I guess it's baptism by fire."

"I'm sure I can handle it."

"Look, Tony, I don't mean any disrespect, but even Lisa – who has been anchoring weekends for about a year – has her hands full with this job. Anyway, give me the motion picture film you shot, so I can get it into the soup for you"

Heeding Ron's words, I thought I'd better get cracking and put on my producer's hat. I had timed and produced a newscast once in college, but that was the extent of my producing experience. Even so, I was confident I could map out a sixteen-minute program, which is what you have left when you take time out for sports, weather, and commercials. I decided, even though the still bust was a big story, my lead story of the newscast would be a twenty-five second copy story on a fatal fire in our viewing area, even though we had no film footage.

Before I knew it, it was 4:30, an hour and a half 'till show time. Ron yelled from the processing room, "Come and get your film, fresh out of the soup!"

Time to put on my editor's hat. I stood at the editing station, screening my film and then cutting and splicing it. The next step would be putting it on a master reel that I would then hand off to the studio projectionist on my way to the studio.

5:31. A lanky, middle-aged man with curly hair and a snickering smile enters the newsroom. "Howdy, Bub. You must be Mr. Paganini."

"Hi. Actually Pagnotti, but call me Tony. You're my director?"

"Yeah, I guess you can call me that. I'm Jack Lawrence. Now, I've seen some of your reports during the week, but have you ever anchored before?"

"Not really. But I did read news copy from a tele-prompter during my college TV internship."

"Well, I see we have a budding Walter Cronkite in our midst."

5:50. After marking the camera shots on the scripts, Jack took his copy and told me to drop off the chroma key slides and film with the projectionist upstairs and then follow the spiral staircase down to the studio, where a cameraman will put a mike on me and then cue me during the newscast. Maybe it was because I was so busy for the past eight hours, I didn't have time to get nervous.

5:55. But now with five minutes to go before my anchor debut I started feeling a few butterflies fluttering in my gut. Just as I was about to hand the film to the projectionist, the tray with about twenty chroma slides, placed in chronological order, tumbled from my hand and fell all over the floor.

I tried frantically to put them back in order, but the projectionist said, "Son, you better get downstairs. Two minutes 'till air time." With that I went flying down the staircase and simultaneously my scripts went flying from my hand. I picked up the pages, opened the studio door and heard a voice shout, "*30 seconds to air. Get in your chair and put your mike on.*" No sooner did I flop into the anchor chair, than the music started to play: *This is Dateline News, the weekend edition.* Red light on. The camera man forcefully thrust a finger in my direction.

"*Good evening, everyone, I'm Tony Pagnotti. Our top story on Dateline news tonight... Early morning fires in Marshall County (eh-ah-eh)...*" Have you ever run extremely fast and then realized you're out of breath? That was me, but it was happening on live TV. "*The blaze broke out* (ehahha ahe)..." The harder I tried to get the words out, the more I was sucking for air. I was thinking, *go to a commercial. Jack, do something. Jack.* But there was nowhere to run or hide. With each shallow breath I took reading the fire story from hell, I saw my TV career going up in smoke. I somehow made it to the next story, a network report, which would give me 1:45 in studio to get my breath back. As I focused and was getting my breath and composure back, Jack announced over the studio intercom, "Hey, I just got a call up here in master control from a viewer, wanting to know if that new Eyetalian guy anchoring the news was having a heart attack? 5, 4,3,2,1... and, cue him."

After the disastrous start, I made it through the rest of half hour relatively unscathed, despite stumbling over a few words here and there. I headed back to the newsroom with the realization that maybe being an anchor wasn't as easy as it looked.

The only sign of life in the newsroom was a ringing phone. Could it be the same viewer who called during the news to see if I had returned to regular cardiac rhythm? "Hello, Dateline news...Tony... yes."

"It was Walt. "What happened? Why you were unable to breathe tonight?"

"Well, you see, I dropped my slides and script."

"Look, we'll take about this first thing Monday. But I got a call from our General Manager who said he was at a party with our news on, when you started gasping. He said he was humiliated and wanted me to fire you, tonight. But I took up for you, big guy. Just come see me in my office on Monday morning."

I spent the rest of the weekend sulking in my apartment, humiliated over the "breathless" performance. Would my baptism by fire end in my being fired? I felt much better after my meeting with Walt. He told me he had calmed down the GM, assuring him it wouldn't happen again. I wouldn't be anchoring again anytime in the near future.

As months passed, I found I was developing a following around Asheville. I found a niche in doing feel-good people stories. I profiled Sister Mary Margaret, an adorable blind, elderly nun who ran a ham radio operator station from the convent. And there were the fun features in which I was always an active participant. When the circus came to town, I rode an elephant and got to dress up like a clown. Whether it was in the grocery store, bank, or post office, I would get a big southern "HEY, TONY" from the down home Ashevillians. There is indeed a rush of importance and pride that a TV broadcaster gets when he's recognized out in public. With that notoriety usually comes special VIP treatment. I knew my star was rising when the manager of *Weiner King* told me he was such a big fan that, whenever I came in to enjoy the best dawgs in town, the meal was on him. Prior to my TV career, I wasn't exactly what you would call a chick magnet but I discovered how being perceived as a local star caused my appeal to the female to flourish. There was something alluring about the stereotypical southern belle: wholesome, charming, innocent, lovely. That description certainly applied to a young lady just about my age, Maggie, whom I got to know doing stories at where she worked at city hall.

When I asked her out on a date, she was apparently thrilled. We went to the local favorite restaurant *The Hot Shot*, where we talked and laughed for a long time. I asked if she would like to stop by for a drink at my deluxe garage apartment.

"Ok, maybe just one," she replied, blushing.

One drink led to two and, before you know it, we were lying in bed, whispering, laughing and cuddling. Then we were startled. The phone rang. Who could be calling this time of the night?

"Hi, big guy, sorry to wake you. Walt here. Just got a call that the Hendersonville Volunteers are at a house fire and there may be one toasted. Huh? You know, possibly a fatal. Need to you get out there ASAP while there are still some flames to get on camera."

"Okay,10-4. On my way."

I apologized to Maggie and told her I'd be back in an hour or so. But then she asked if she could come along, since she had never been on the scene of a fire. So, off we went. With news camera in hand, we went past the onlookers and up to the house. Walt would be happy that there were still enough flames shooting from the roof to make my fiery footage show how quick Dateline News is on spot news coverage. As I hustled around the dwelling, zooming in and out to get different angles of the scene, I asked a fireman who I had just shot dousing the blaze, "Hey, I was wondering if you could confirm that there is one dead?"

"Yeah, Tony, there is. And if you don't be careful where you step, you'll be able to confirm that firsthand, or, should I say. First foot.

Looking down, only a few feet away was what looked to be a large chunk of smoldering firewood. It was my first, and, unfortunately, not my last, up-close-and-personal look at a dead person. I felt sick and saddened. "Come on, Maggie, let's get out of here."

As we turned and headed back to the news car, the fireman yelled, "Hey, Tony, when are you going to put all the good pictures you took on the news?"

It was a quiet ride back from the fire. Maggie had fallen asleep and I was doing a lot of thinking about how much I liked being on TV and telling human interest stories. But today had shown me that I sure didn't have the heart, or stomach, for reporting on human tragedy or misfortune. I woke Maggie as we were approaching her parent's house where she lived. I apologized for the way our fun date ended, but she acknowledged that's what it was like when you date a newsman. After a quick kiss goodnight, I headed back to my place with mixed feelings of guilt and depression.

You see, there was something I wanted to tell Maggie but didn't get around to. In just a few months, I would be going back home to Pennsylvania to get married. It seemed like a good idea to get engaged to my college girlfriend, Barbara, during our last year of school. Not knowing where, or if, I ever would get a job after graduation, we had decided love would see us through, and a May wedding was planned.

When WLOS came calling a few months later, Barbara had to stay behind in Pennsylvania to attend graduate school. No problem, I assured her, go ahead and make the wedding plans, and I'll call every day from Asheville with updates.

For the first month that had worked, but then I found myself being more wrapped up in honing my TV skills than I was caring about what kind of wedding cake we should order.

I found myself eating, living, and sleeping TV, which had me wondering if I would have the time or devotion necessary to be a loving husband. But I felt it was too late to turn back.

I would go ahead with the plan and hope it would all work out. When I told Walt that I was getting married, he gave me a big handshake and smile. But his look quickly changed when I said that I would need a week off to get married and go on a brief honeymoon.

"Oh, I would love to, big guy, but I have no one to fill in for four days. And, you know, we'll still be in the heart of ratings. At best, I can try and get you three days."

Barbara wasn't pleased but I told her that, if I demanded the time off, I wouldn't have a job to come back to. I promised we could go on a delayed honeymoon on our first anniversary. So, after a four-day hiatus to get married, I returned to WLOS, minus my bride – who would be staying in PA until she got her graduate degree. I pulled into the station with a new 1976 Buick, thanks to a generous gift from my parents. I was ready to get back to work. I thought, *I haven't been on TV for nearly a week.* It was a beautiful sunny day in the Land of the Sky, but, upon entering the station, there seemed to be a big, dark cloud hanging over the newsroom.

The usually lively receptionist Priscilla looked up and, forcing a smile, said "Welcome back, married man."

"Why the gloom?"

Rolling her eyes, she said, "You'll see."

In the newsroom, my six colleagues were sitting around, looking like they lost their best friends. Noticeably missing was Walt Adams. I turned to Billings and asked where Walt was.

"He's been shit-canned."

Then, all eyes were directed toward the tall, good-looking man in his early thirties, bearing a big smile. He greeted us. "Hello, everyone, my name is Bill Boyer. I'm a consultant for the *Masters Research Company*." With an air of cockiness, he continued, "Your general manager hired our firm to help turn this TV station into the highest-rated operation in the Tar Heel state. To begin with, we recommended that, in order for that to happen, we needed new leadership. We will help in that search. Walt Adams is no longer with the station." My heart sank. How could they do that to Walt? He had a wife, two kids and mortgage on a beautiful home that he loved so much. How could they unceremoniously fire a guy who was hard-working and did the best he could with an inexperienced staff and limited resources?

"Until we hire a new news director, I'll be here to assign stories and work with you individually to make you better TV journalists. I've watched tapes of your past few months of newscasts so I can give you specific critiques and recommendations. Now, let's go out there, team, and do good TV!"

I had a fun feature story to do that day on Ben and Billy McGuire from nearby Swannanoa, who were in the Guinness Book as the world's fattest twins, weighing 720 pounds each. My on-camera standup ended with the guys' arms tightly wrapped around me. Turning to the camera with a big cheesy chuckle , I concluded: "Talk about making a baloney sandwich. I'm Tony Pagnotti, Dateline News."

Later that afternoon as I was screening and editing my story, I was thinking how Bill Boyer would love the story, since consultants are big on the *"Hey Martha"* stories, along with creative reporter involvement. I was almost finished, when I looked up and saw Bill standing next to me. "Got a minute?"

I followed him outside the newsroom to the hallway. With a very stern look he said, "You know, not everyone is cut out to be on TV. Before taking this job, did you consider any other career paths? In looking over your work, I thought I should give you my honest assessment."

Dumbfounded and crushed, I didn't say I word.

He then extended his hand and, with a mock look of sincerity, said, "Think about it."

I'm not sure why, but I shook his hand and said, "OK."

I went back to finish my editing, but felt so blindsided and numb. I handed my script and film story to the producer and headed for the door.

"Tony, where you going, aren't you going to stay and watch the Six with the rest of us?"

"No. I'm not feeling well."

I got back to my apartment and threw myself on the bed. How could he say that to me? What was so bad about me that he would tell me to get out of TV? Did he really mean it, or maybe it was the GM who wanted me to follow in the footsteps of the recently departed news director? If I quit TV, there was nothing else I knew how to do, or even wanted to do. How could I go home and explain that, sometimes, happy lottery winners experience misfortune? I couldn't think straight. I closed my eyes and cried myself to sleep.

The next morning I wasn't sure I could go back into work and face the man who told me to pull the plug on what I felt was a budding TV career. But as it turned out, I didn't have that encounter. When I walked into the newsroom, producer Charles Mann said he was news director for the time being, explaining that Boyer had had to return to his corporate office in Texas. Charles would now be in charge of the day-to-day operation until the new news director was hired.

After I grabbed his hand and gave him a big pat on his back, Charles chuckled. "Tony, I don't know if that means you're glad for me or glad that Bill Boyer has left the building."

I grinned and thought, *if he only knew.*

If there was any good to come out of the advice given to me by Bad News Bill, it was the realization that, if you're going to make it as a TV personality, you've got to believe in yourself and not allow yourself to be derailed.. I knew that in less than a year in the business, I was making a name for myself in Asheville. I could have taken the advice from the so-called expert and packed it in. But what also dawned on me was how random, subjective and unfair firings could be. I saw how news directors and anchors lived and died by the ratings books. As the eternal pessimist Billings (who more and more was sounding like a realist to me) once told me, "This is a business of paranoid, insecure people who live by the mantra, 'here today gone tomorrow.'"

That's why I reasoned so many of my colleagues were sending out tapes and resumes looking for new jobs. There is no loyalty to a present employer. There was a need to be ready to move on to another station in the event that the axe unexpectedly came falling down on you. So, I decided it was time to troll the waters of the vast ocean that is local TV news. With a resume tape highlighting my capabilities, I was hoping to make a big splash in a bigger pond. And I would begin fishing back in the classified pages of *Broadcasting Magazine.*

Given my limited experience, I knew I wasn't ready yet for stations in the Top 20 markets. Over the course of the month, I applied for reporter positions in Jacksonville, Phoenix, Sacramento, Providence, Kansas City and Columbus. I can't say my confidence was bolstered when I got either rejection letters or no responses at all. But, I knew from past experience that no matter how many times I played, I only needed one winning ticket to cash in on the TV lottery. So, in the meantime, while I waited for lady luck to hit, I would enjoy the present and the new two-bedroom apartment that I'd moved into in anticipation of my new wife joining me in a few months. And while you may wonder why I was looking to leave town when my wife and I were to begin our married life together, I can only say this: TV types aren't the most rational or logical thinkers in the world.

As fate would have it, two months after Barbara arrived and found a job as a speech pathologist in Asheville, I got a call of interest from WTVN-TV 6 in Columbus, Ohio. The news director flew me in for an interview, told me how much he liked my creative style and on-camera presence, and said that he would like to offer me a reporter's position. I told him I was flattered that he was interested but didn't know if the timing was right, considering my wife and I had just settled into Asheville. I didn't want to uproot unless I thought it was the right move for me. From across his desk, he said, "Well, you will be moving up to the thirty-fourth TV market. You will have a photographer shoot and edit all your stories with state-of-the-art video cameras, and you'll be making two hundred and fifty bucks a week."

Trying not to convey my innermost "wow" reaction, I asked if he could give me a few days to talk it over with my wife.

"Sure, but I need to hear back from you no later than Friday." And he sneered and pointed over to a stack of about fifty resume tapes that I assumed belonged to other candidates also hoping to win the Columbus lottery.

On the plane ride home, I was thinking I had to take it. Like George and Weezie of *The Jeffersons*, I would be moving on up. In addition to working in a top thirty-five market, I would be making ninety more bucks a week, which would mean five grand more a year.

"Are you crazy? I just moved here to begin our marriage; I just got a great job in my field, not to mention we have ten months to go on our apartment lease!" It wasn't exactly the reaction I was hoping for from the woman I was supposed to be spending the rest of my life with.

"I hear everything you're saying, but opportunities like these are so few and far between that, if I turn it down, I might be here in Asheville another year before I get an interview, let alone another job offer."

With tears she asked what my priorities in life were, anyway. I stood silently as she walked away.

I tossed and turned and tried to figure out why I would allow my marriage to get off on the wrong foot, just so I could put my foot in the next rung of the TV ladder. Or was I feeling that I could be making nearly ten thousand dollars more a year on what I envisioned was one step closer to stardom? With one day to go to make a decision before the Columbus offer was off the table, I had a compromise to offer my wife.

"What about this, Barbara? I'll take the job, and you stay here in Asheville for the next six months and work 'till the end of the year, with the plan that you fly to Columbus once a month so we can see each other. I could get settled in Columbus and find us a nice apartment. You always said you eventually want to get your Master's. Well, Ohio State's Columbus campus has a great grad school in speech pathology. What do you think?"

She paused and replied, "Okay, if it means that much to you."

After a nice farewell party thrown by my TV-13 colleagues and a warning from Billings, "You're making a big mistake, I hear that Channel 6 Columbus is a bigger dump than here," I felt like I was being called up from "A" ball in the minors to the AAA league. Carolina was no longer on my mind.

4

GOODBYE CAROLINA, HELLO COLUMBUS. (1978)

The newsroom staff at TV 6 ACTION NEWS was double the size of WLOS. The reporters, anchors and photographers had anywhere from two to twenty years of experience in the business and turned out a much more professional and polished product than what I was used to at TV 13. Working with a seasoned videographer certainly helped make reporters' news stories network quality. I also found that, once I reached the level of mid-market TV, news directors became hands-off administrators. The day-to-day news product was now in the hands of executive producers, producers and assignment editors, which are known in mass communications as the "gatekeepers." These folks, along with the reporters, had a meeting each morning to decide what got covered and what didn't make the night's newscast. The big question to be answered at these meetings was what we were going to lead with that night. That was an easy decision if there was a fire, murder, or another crime story that happened in the area. Beyond that, priority would be given to city government and stories of local economic impact such as a business shutting down, resulting in job losses. Rounding out the fare would be the "Hey, Martha" feature stories, which were also called "human interest."

I often wondered if there were any forms of life other than humans watching TV news. It was at these meetings where I first discovered the insensitivity and sometimes ghoulish attitudes of the gatekeepers.

I'll never forget the first time I heard our gruff assignment editor, Hal Fenton, frustrated there was no lead story for the day, say, "I just hope that, sometime before 6 o'clock tonight, a plane goes down over OSU or that a six-alarmer rips through the Harman Housing projects."

To my astonishment, as I looked around the table, there were nods of agreement. This wouldn't be the last time in my career that this type of conversation would be repeated. I discovered that the news business often attracts self-proclaimed news junkies who are aware that live, local and late-breaking stories of human tragedy translate into big news ratings. I felt almost like an outsider, since my desire to get into TV news wasn't driven by breaking news of death or destruction. I'm still not sure what the driving force was, but it certainly wasn't the rush received from being able to document and then broadcast human misfortune or tragedy. I'm not certain if former Eagles vocalist Don Henley either worked in TV news or knew someone who did, but he certainly captured the parasitic nature of the business in his solo 1981 rock hit *Dirty Laundry:*

I make my living off the TV News
Give me something I can use
We love it when you lose
Give us dirty laundry

The one big downside that I found in moving up in TV market size was that the bigger the city, the more frequent the occurrence of spot news and crime stories. I must say that, in my first few months at Channel 6, I covered more such stories than I did during my entire year spent in Asheville. I didn't enjoy doing fires, murders and the like, but I knew it came with the reportorial territory.

I found that one way to avoid those hard-news assignments was to come up with enterprising feature stories. My sense of satisfaction came from doing what are commonly called "Good News" stories. I had developed a niche for taking ordinary people and events and turning them into positive slices of everyday life. But, as I found out each time I tried to pitch my stories, it wasn't an easy sell. When you're up against the gatekeeper mentality "if it bleeds, it leads," those feel-good stories often fell into the "evergreen" category – meaning it would be taped but would not air until there was a slow news day. But being given such low priority didn't bother me, because I knew that if I grew enough evergreens they would eventually be harvested from the forest and see the light of day on the evening news.

Among the human interest stories I started gravitating toward were those involving disabled people who were inspirational in their achievements. Despite the great viewer response I would get from such stories, many of my hard-news-minded colleagues had more cynical responses. When a story is scheduled to be reported, the assignment editor writes a two- or three-word caption for each story (called the slug) up on the big board for producers to see what stories were scheduled for that night's newscast. The slug would then be typed onto all of the scripts. Since the viewing public never sees the slug chosen for the story, producers would delight in making up some inappropriate captions.

For instance, my story on a visually impaired woman who enjoyed Triple A Columbus Clippers baseball by taking in the sounds of the game was slugged *BLIND AS A BAT.* The heartwarming feature on a man who was a quadriplegic but produced wonderful works of art using a mouth stick brush was slugged *TARD ART.*

Even though I had to grin and bear the sophomoric newsroom humor, I had the last laugh when both stories were picked up by our ABC network, distributed to affiliate stations and broadcast in cities around the country. It was also quite a personal career milestone, since it marked the first time my parents had the chance to see their son on TV. When WNEP, my hometown TV station where I interned, showed my features on the 6 PM news, my proud mama taped the segments on her VCR and made it must-see-TV for anyone who entered her house. Another TV first for me in Columbus was doing what are called in the biz "live shots". That's when the anchor in the studio introduces the reporter who is standing by live at one location.

We didn't have the required live microwave vans in Asheville, so all my reports there were pre-recorded. That meant a reporter could redo his story if he made a mistake or wasn't pleased with the first take. When you're live, you must get it right the first time. No retakes. So you could imagine my trepidation the first time in Columbus I had to do a live shot. There I was, standing out among the crowds gathered in the midway of the Ohio state fair, wearing an earpiece connected to a small electronic box hidden in my back pants pocket. A producer back in the station control room barked *standby one minute*. That triggered two thoughts: first, what happens if I mess up and forget what I'm supposed to say? Second, guess it's too late for me to go take a quick pee?

Action news reporter Tony Pagnotti is standing by live having fun at the midway at the state fair. Tony, are you going to bring us back some cotton candy?

In my ear, I heard the director say, *cut to Tony, cue Tony.*

Without missing a beat, I replied, *"You bet, Earl. I'll be sure to bring back some cotton candy and corn dogs."* You'll often hear that type of exchange between anchor and reporter on location. News directors like it because the impromptu chatter reminds the viewer that this is live television and has not been taped earlier. It also conveys camaraderie between members of the news team. In reality, even though a reporter says he will bring back the anchors this or that, ninety-nine percent of the time he doesn't make good on his on-air promise. My reasoning was, why would I want to spend five bucks or so for my colleague who might be a nice guy or gal, but who is also making about three times more than I am?

It was that kind of anchor envy that got me thinking about ways to obtain in-studio experience, which would lead to someday becoming the better paid and more prestigious anchorman. Toward that end, I wrote a proposal/suggestion to my news director saying that the noon news would be a lot livelier if solo anchor Annie Papa had a male partner sitting next to her. As the old saying goes, timing is everything, because the news director sent me a memo (no emails in those days) that he, too, felt the noon show should have a co-anchor, but that he didn't have money in the budget to hire one.

I darted down to his office and said, "You don't have to hire a noon co-anchor." I explained that I could go out and cover news stories in the morning or late afternoon so I could always be in the studio at noon to co-anchor.

"Hey that's a great idea, but one problem: Have you ever anchored?"

"Oh, yeah, in Asheville". As a broadcast journalist, I believe in full disclosure, just not when it comes to getting a chance to take a giant step up the TV news ladder at the age of 25.

"All right, let's give it a shot on Monday and see how it goes. But you do realize you will still be making your same reporter salary."

"I understand." As I thought, I would have to take a small pay cut to enter the world of *anchordom*. And even though many of my fellow reporters congratulated me, I detected some resentment from those who had more experience but were passed over for the anchor job.

Despite my one-time breathless anchor performance in Asheville, I felt surprisingly calm as I took my place on the set next to my dark-haired, heavily made-up partner Anita who had a reputation as what's known as a "reader". With very little or no reporting experience, "readers" are paid for their good looks and smooth delivery.

Reading stories in tandem from the rolling teleprompter and bantering cheerfully to lead into weather and sports, our co-anchor debut got positive reviews in the newsroom. Of course, our Don Rickles of the newsroom, Hal Fenton, yelled across the newsroom, "Hey, we should promote Papa and Pagnotti as the Double Dego hour, bringing you 'Wop news at noon.'" The News Director was pleased, saying that the show flowed and there was a nice chemistry between Anita and me. His one suggestion was to get some pancake makeup to cover beard shadows and blemishes under the harsh studio lights. I went to the drugstore and bought my first Maybelline makeup, which helps an anchorman put his best face forward.

My entry into the anchor world gave me my first shot at one of the big perks in such a high-profile position: the chance to meet and interview famous people. In Columbus, The Ohio Theater was home to touring Broadway shows. Promoters would make the stars available to local news media. I remember how excited I would be on those days when celebrity interviews were scheduled with the star of that week's show. I brought along my own Polaroid camera once, so I could get a picture standing next to the lovable, pint-sized iconic actor Mickey Rooney. This would be the first of many experiences in my career where the celeb didn't measure up to his or her film or TV persona. When Mickey entered the interview room, he certainly didn't have that lovable and happy-go-lucky demeanor he portrayed on the silver screen. When I introduced myself, Mickey didn't even crack a cordial smile. As my photographer placed a mike on him, I told the diminutive legend how much I loved his movies.

He barely acknowledged my statement. "I got to get back to rehearsal; this is only going to be a few minutes, right?" he barked.

"Yes, sir." Then, as soon as my camera man started rolling and cued us, a very recognizable big grin came over Mickey's face and he started answering my questions like we were best friends. After the interview, he quickly got up from his chair, halfheartedly saying thanks. As he reached for the door, I was about to ask if he had a second to take a picture with me. But before I could ask, he was gone in a flash. Maybe the star of stage and screen abruptly ended the interview fearing this reporter would ask him about his eight wives.

As we had planned, Barbara moved to Columbus and we finally began living together in the same state. She soon discovered one big drawback of being married to a TV newsman: he doesn't work a routine nine-to-five shift. Besides a regular diet of nights and weekends, the holidays are spent away from home. Thanksgiving, Christmas, and Easter celebrations would have to happen around my work schedule.

Before enrolling in Ohio State's graduate program, Barbara asked me to promise that I wouldn't be looking for a new job, at least until she earned her Master's degree. I kept my promise over the next few months, but then, unexpectedly, a great job possibility somehow found me. An old friend and college classmate John Kosinski called to tell me that in his hometown of New Haven, Connecticut, the ABC station was looking for a weekend anchor-reporter. What the heck, I thought, it wouldn't hurt to send a tape, just to test the waters of the eighteenth market. It's even located less than an hour from New York City, the number one market in the land.

But testing the TV waters was beginning to test the stability of my marriage. Barbara startled me when she told me, "If you get the job in New Haven, you will be moving there by yourself." With that warning, I almost hoped I would never hear from TV 8. But as fate would have it, another winning lottery ticket was about to land in my hand. The New Haven interview resulted in a three-year contract offer, starting at $25,000 and reaching $30,000 in the last year.

How could I say no?

5

GOODBYE COLUMBUS, HELLO NEW HAVEN (1979)

New city, familiar routine. Barbara, true to her word, would stay behind and finish her Master's degree and I would climb up several more rungs of the TV ladder to quickly become a prime-time weekend anchor. As part of my contract agreement, the station said it would put me up in the nearby Sheraton, where all my meals were included. In addition to my salary and benefits, I felt I was now in the big leagues, having my own producer Jonathon Leveen who selected the stories, wrote most of the copy, and timed the half hour newscast. My main responsibility was to read smoothly from the teleprompter and ad lib witty banter with the weather and sports guys.

Besides being weekend anchor, I was a general assignment reporter three days a week. One day I could be covering a school board meeting or a fire, and the next day my story would be perhaps a murder or maybe a human interest story on a 100-year-old's birthday party. I was quickly discovering that in TV news, the cities may change, but the predictable stories remain the same. There seemed to be an unwritten formula for covering a given story. For instance, news managers always felt it was a real coup if, when covering a murder, the photographer got the victim being carted off in a body bag to a waiting ambulance. Then, it was up to the hardnosed reporter to seek out a family member or someone who knew the deceased, it didn't matter who, to provide a grief-stricken interview. I hated that part of the job, but knew that, if I didn't capture the human misery on tape, when I got back to the station I would face a berating by my boss.

Failure to produce that dirty laundry was a well-known cause for disciplinary action and even getting fired. So, maybe it was because of that increased pressure, in addition to the added stress of the large markets to always get the highest ratings, that after-work-partying increased proportionality with market size.

After the 11 PM newscasts, it was common in New Haven for the staff to get together at a colleague's house to blow off a little steam. The first time I went to one of these parties, I found myself quite surprised. When I walked into the house, my colleague, who just an hour earlier was doing a live shot from the police station where he was reporting on local drug bust, was now in his living room puffing on a joint and passing it around the table. Up to now, the only time I'd tried marijuana was a few times in college.

"Come on, Pagman, join the party!" shouted a few of my colleagues.

It didn't take much persuading. I took a seat on the sofa and took a toke of the wacky weed while the funny cigarette made the rounds. Soon enough, I came down with the giggles, thinking of what would happen if the New Haven police busted the pot party. Would all of us be doing a live remote Action News 8 broadcast from the city jail? Fortunately, there was no broadcaster's bust that night.

New Haven also gave me my first interview with a national political figure. Ted Kennedy, who had just announced he was entering the Democratic Presidential Primary, was making a swing through town. Local media outlets were told that one of their reporters would be allowed a five-minute taped Q and A with the iconic legislator. I lobbied hard for the plum assignment and got it.

Fellow reporter and good friend Reggie Harris came by my desk as I was getting ready to head out to meet the Senator. "Wow. Pag, I'm jealous. This will look awesome on your resume tape. A one-on-one with the King of the Kennedys. This is the kind of story that news directors in New York City look for when they're searching for reporters. So make it network quality."

As I was waiting my turn at the hotel, a press person for the Senator came over to remind me that I had only five minutes of the candidate's valuable time and that the only questions Ted would answer were those regarding the present campaign. Translation: don't kick Kennedy in his Achilles Heel and ask him about his infamous behavior at Chappaquiddick. The story is well known. In 1972, after a night of drinking at the Kennedy compound in Hyannis Port, Ted and a young female staffer were driving along a back road nearing the Chappaquiddick Bridge when the car veered into the river. The Senator, unable to find his companion in the water, swam back to shore and didn't report what happened until the morning. The woman, Mary Jo Kopechne, drowned. The question now sweeping the country was if America would be willing to elect a man who made such a deadly mistake.

An unsmiling, craggy-faced Senator entered the room and shook my hand while my camera man rolled the tape. I tossed Ted some softball questions about his hopes for the campaign. He knocked those out of the park with a studied sincerity, a smile and a charming Boston accent. With my slotted interview time running out, I decided to go for it and hit him where it hurt... in the Achilles heel.

Senator, do you think the American public is willing to forgive and forget Chappaquiddick and elect you president?

Pausing for a second before replying, the disgusted and angry-looking Senator shook his head and said, "I am not going to discuss that."

As soon as I concluded the interview and said thank you, Senator Kennedy was whisked out the door. On that evening's news, I was the only New Haven TV reporter to ask the tough question. The Kennedy segment would make news directors in New York sit up and take note of my resume tape. But there was no time to think about my lifelong dream of being on TV in the Big Apple, because my wife was on her way to town to catch up again with her traveling TV husband.

For the first time in our dysfunctional marriage, things were settling down for the two of us. We rented a walk-up brownstone in the city's Little Italy neighborhood where some of the greatest pizza, Italian food, and bakeries could be found. I was feeling pretty good about life, making good money in a high-profile anchor-reporter position for friendly town located sixty miles away from the city that never sleeps. But, as I would come to learn through the years, don't allow yourself to become too comfortable or complacent in the cutthroat world of TV. The newsroom secretary told me that news director Steve Craig wanted to see me. When I walked in, he was holding a copy of my contract. Cutting to the chase, he looked me straight in the eye and said,

"We have decided to exercise the option of not picking up the remaining two years on your contract."

"What?"

"Under the terms of the agreement, the station can give you sixty days' notice of termination."

"So, you're telling me that, two months from now, I'm out of a job?"

"Yes, that's right."

"Why?"

"As your lawyer probably pointed out to you when you signed the contract, no reason needs to be given for termination. The station has decided to hire a new weekend anchor-reporter."

I guess I'd never read the fine print and only saw the big bucks spelled out in the document. Not to mention, I hadn't felt the need at the time to consult with an attorney over an agreement that I naively assumed was etched in stone. I didn't have it in me to tell Barbara that, through no fault of my own, I had to start looking for a new job in a new town. When I contacted the other TV stations in Connecticut, I was told by news managers that they liked my work a lot, but there were no openings. They would keep me in mind. What bothered me most was that I had no idea why I was being fired from TV 8. My colleagues were all surprised and very supportive of me when they heard of my imminent departure. Many of them said my release was a reminder of why paranoia runs rampant in TV stations around the country.

One day, the staff's loveable, veteran videographer who shot from the hip, John Mongillo, a New Haven native in his sixties, pulled me aside. "Look, kid, I think these bastards here are fuckin' you over. But I heard something through the grapevine that I thought you should hear. The GM's wife is the reason you're getting shit-canned. Yeah, my sources tell me that from the day you was hired here she kept telling her old man that she didn't like your looks or style."

I couldn't believe what Monge was telling me. He concluded, "Frankly da bitch is a blue blood who looks down on wops, especially one like you, being' on her hubby's station."

Could a prejudiced woman have that much influence over her husband's business decisions? I felt hurt, but I knew I had to move forward. Such is the nature of TV.

Viewers get to know their TV friends and welcome them into their homes every night. But sometimes viewers notice members of that electronic family have gone missing. Sometimes, the anchor or reporter gets the chance in a final farewell to say he will miss the great town of Whatever, America, but now he has the chance to pursue a new and challenging career opportunity. But in my case, like many other TV departures, we are in their homes one day and gone the next.

In my first weeks of being unemployed, I spent a lot of time at the local post office, mailing resume tapes to stations all over the country. *Have tapes, will travel.* There were the usual rejections or no responses at all. There were calls to former colleagues with whom I had worked to see if they knew of any job leads. One of my friends Tom Weldon asked if I had filed for unemployment compensation yet. I hadn't even thought about it, but was eligible to collect 200 dollars a week. With only Barbara's paycheck coming in, I knew I had to get some additional revenue to compensate for my lost wages. So, off I went to the local unemployment office, a place I had been many times before, as a TV reporter doing new stories. The lines were long and I held up a newspaper to my face, hoping that my recognizable mug wouldn't be seen. But two lines over I saw two young men pointing in my direction and yelling for all to hear, "Hey, that looks like Tony Pagnotti, Action News. Hey, man, where's your cameraman, you doing a story on all us folks who don't have a J-O-B.?"

The lady in front of me turned around and said, "Are you Tony Pagnotti?"

To which I sheepishly replied, "I used to be," and buried my face back in the newspaper.

The experience was a dose of reality on how suddenly one can go from a prestigious, well-paying job to the unemployment line. I was served another giant piece of humility pie when I decided to fill up my free time by volunteering at the New Haven Soup Kitchen. Twice a week, I'd don an apron and serve lunch to the homeless. As I soon discovered, most of the folks I served weren't the stereotypical mentally ill drug addicts incapable of working. During candid conversations, I heard hard luck stories from a wide variety of people, including a formerly successful businessman and a college professor who never dreamed he would wind up in such dire financial straits. Before the grace of God go I.

During my networking calls, I reached out to my old pal John Kosinski. After graduating from BU he began working as a TV news consultant for *Primo People Inc.* in nearby Old Greenwich, CT. The firm's founder, Al Primo, was the renowned creator of the Eyewitness News concept back in the late 60s. When I met with John, he promised to peddle my tape to their client stations around the country. Al told me he had seen my work and was impressed. When I told him that I didn't know why I was canned at TV 8, he said that I should put that in my past and be more concerned about landing a new gig. Then, looking me straight in the eye, he said, "Don't sit at home and wait for your phone to ring. See if any local radio or TV stations have any part-time work available. In this business, you need to be doing something, not just sitting on the sidelines and waiting. If you don't stay active, you'll soon fade to dust." Words of wisdom from a TV news legend.

When I left his office, I forced myself to stop by a small, low-budget UHF station in Waterbury: CT Channel 24. It was the only station I hadn't contacted because, frankly, I thought it was a bush-league operation, paying bush league wages. My suspicions were confirmed when I pulled up to a trailer with a small worn circular sign outside it reading "TV 24". I almost turned around but Al's wise advice caused me to move forward knocking on the trailer door, when I walked in, a preety young blonde woman Debbie Hanley greeted me. "Tony Pagnotti what are you doing here? I watched you on Channel 8 all the time and wondered what happened to you."

I explained my contract wasn't renewed and was wondering if Channel 24 had any openings.

"Well," she said, "I'm the news director and anchor of our 6 o'clock news and it just so happens that our sports guy just left. Are you interested?"

"Well, I am a sports fan, but have never been a sports anchor."

"I should tell you it's a part-time, twenty-hour-week position. We'd love to have such a well-known celebrity here at our itty-bitty operation." Itty-bitty was an accurate description of the room which served as the bare bones un-heated studio. "I am also embarrassed to tell you that the position only pays six bucks an hour," which, in 1981 was just a few bucks above the minimum wage.

I almost said, "thanks, but no, thanks," but then I realized this decision wasn't about money; it was a chance to be back on TV, albeit in a very diminished capacity. "Okay, when would you need me to start?"

"How about tomorrow?"

So, from a very cramped, unglamorous trailer, I was the new sports anchor at TV 24. I had fun being back on the air, often wondering how many people were actually watching this station with its traditionally anemic ratings. I was barely making enough money to pay for the gas needed to get to and from work, but the job certainly gave my sagging confidence a real boost. From time to time, a few stations where I had sent tapes would respond, but there was no real interest. Then, a few months later, I came home and checked the messages on my answering machine.

"Hi, I'm looking for Tony Pagnotti. This is Jack Phillips at WNBC-News 4, New York. I liked the tape you sent me a while back and wanted to talk to you about a reporter's position we have here." I played it over and over and then thought I should speed dial 911 because I thought I was about to have a heart attack.

Two days later and there I was, standing in front of 30 Rockefeller Center, looking up at the iconic building where I was about to be interviewed for a job at NBC's number one flagship station. As I rode the elevator up to the sixth floor, the door opened and in came NBC anchorman Tom Brokaw and Today Show host Bryant Gumbal. I tried maintaining my cool and resisted the urge to ask for autographs.

At the start of the interview, Phillips made it clear that the reporters position he had was only guaranteed for six months since one of his reporters was leaving to have a baby and expected to return to her post after maternity leave. But he also pointed out that, if she decided not to return to work, I could be in line to be hired full time. He said that, of the hundreds of tapes he viewed, my on-camera charisma and creative style caught his eye. He also said I should thank Reggie Harris, my pal from New Haven, who was now a reporter at WNBC. He said Reggie fished my tape from the stacks of resume reels piled in his office and made sure the news director watched it. Then, Phillips matter-of-factly stated that the salary would be $50,000 a year. I inwardly gulped thinking this would be the ultimate winning lottery ticket.

We shook hands. My first day of work at News 4 NY would be in two weeks. As I was leaving the building, I looked back up at the imposing structure which would be my new workplace. I laughed, giddily thinking about my reversal of fortune, about going from a trailer park in Waterbury making six bucks an hour to the country's number one TV market and pulling in a weekly paycheck of 1000 dollars. On a personal level, this also was fantastic news. Barbara and I would not have to pack up and leave the town and friends we had come to enjoy so much. I would be commuting each day from the New Haven Metro North Station to Grand Central Station in New York. With 15 stops along the way, the trip was an hour and forty-five minutes.

A three-hour, round-trip commute to work sounded taxing, but at least I was guaranteed a job in the country's number one market for at least the next six months.

6

NEW YORK CITY: IF I CAN MAKE IT THERE, I'LL MAKE IT ANYWHERE (1982)

My schedule was 2:30 to 11:30 PM, Wednesday through Sunday, with Mondays and Tuesdays off. I would catch the noon train from New Haven and then catch the last train out from Grand Central at midnight, which would get me home around 2 AM. A grinding schedule, but I reasoned it away as a small price to pay for a chance to play in the big leagues. And working at NEWS 4 NY certainly was a major-league atmosphere. As one of ten reporters, I would be given my story and then assigned to a two-person crew, which consisted of a videographer and sound technician.

In my first week on the job, I quickly learned how versatile a general assignment reporter in NYC must be. For instance, one time I was covering a fatal house fire for the

5 and 6 o'clock news and no sooner had I signed off – *Tony Pagnotti, News 4, the Bronx* – than my assignment editor told my crew and I to grab a quick bite and then head immediately to Central Park. Dianna Ross was giving a free concert and I would be live among the fans for our 11 PM newscast.

Being on the night shift, I got the steady diet of murders, fires, and crime-related stories known as spot news. Unfortunately, I still found that I didn't look forward to doing spot news. I always felt that what I enjoyed most about being on TV was being an entertainer and not an investigative journalist. But I had developed quite an effective formula for cranking out hard news reports to fit any occasion. One mandatory element was compelling video of a crime scene. That was the photographer's job: to capture images depicting the appropriate death, destruction, or devastation. As a reporter, it was my job to seek out the facts and interviews that would illustrate the human tragedy.

If a reporter doesn't deliver the pathos in a story, he or she can expect to face the wrath of a news manager. During newscasts, the News 4 gatekeepers gather in the newsroom and simultaneously watch all of the other news broadcasts. Once, after coming back from a story, I arrived in the newsroom as our six o'clock news was about to begin. The lead story on all the stations was about a teenager who was found shot to death in a Queens's subway station. Every news outlet had the crime scene pictures with the police searching for clues, and the EMS crew taking away the murder victim in a body bag. But then, on Eyewitness ABC 7 news appeared an emotionally distraught mother of the victim crying, "Why would someone do this to my baby?"

No sooner did the anchors say *in other news tonight* than the News director began screaming for the entire newsroom to hear: "DID YOU SEE THAT CHANNEL 7 GOT THE DEAD KID'S MOTHER CRYING? ALL WE HAD WAS THE POLICE SOUNDBITE IN OUR STORY. Get Dave Gilbert, the News 4 reporter, on the phone and tell him to get into my office when he gets back here."

The next day I approached Dave and asked what happened.

He said Phillips asked him if channel 7 got the crying mother, why hadn't he? He was warned that if he got beat on a story again, he would be fired. It was that mentality from management that drove me to chronicle human tragedy, no matter how much it went against my personal beliefs. But playing the role of a gung-ho, hardnosed reporter almost turned me into a victim. My photographer Dean Hart and sound man Nick Mayer, two seasoned members of the press corps, were sent to a Harlem high-rise building, the last known address of a youth gang leader who was arrested for murdering a rival gang member. Our assignment editor said I needed to get some interviews at the complex with anyone who knew him. When the three of us got out of our news car, a group of about fifty people were standing around talking in front of the high rise.

My partner Nick warned, "Make it quick, or we might not have four wheels on our vehicle when we get back to the car."

As I approached people both young and old, it was clear no one wanted to talk on camera about their neighborhood gang leader. But one senior citizen told me that the murder suspect's brother was in his apartment on the sixteenth. *Wow!* I thought, *wouldn't that be a great exclusive, being the only reporter in town who got an interview with the guy's brother?* As I turned to Dean and Nick, they turned away from me and headed for the car. "Hey, where you guys going? We have the chance to interview the brother upstairs in his apartment."

"Sorry, Pal, you're on your own. Our union says we don't have to work in an environment that's potentially unsafe. So, if you get the brother, bring him down here. And we'll be glad to do your interview right outside the car."

Against my better judgment, I entered the building and pushed the up button on the elevator. On my way to the sixteenth floor the rickety elevator stopped on each floor for other residents to get off and on. Some very unwelcoming looks were directed toward me, the big white man in the three-piece suit, who most probably assumed was a member of NYPD. I rang the bell outside 1622 once, twice and three times, but there was no answer. Just as I was about to head toward the elevator, the apartment door flew open, and a young, angry-looking man wearing only shorts yelled, "Get out of here, motherfucker! This is private property."

As I tried to identify myself, his voice became louder and he threatened, "you'll be sorry." then ran back into his apartment. With that, I made a mad dash for the elevator but decided otherwise and headed down the stairwell. I sprinted down all sixteen floors to the news car.

Nick asked with a smirk, "Well, Geraldo Rivera, did you get the brother to talk?"

"No, but you guys need to get out of the car so I can do a standup with the building in the background."

Neighbors here at the Watson high-rise said they knew the murder suspect who lived here but refused to go on-camera for fear of their own safety. Meanwhile, I learned through a source that the gang leader's brother was home tonight. But when I went to his sixteenth-floor apartment, he yelled at me to get off his property and then threatened me by saying "you'll be sorry." I'm Tony Pagnotti, News 4, Harlem.

After that experience, I started thinking how it's surprising that there weren't more incidents where TV news crews were threatened or assaulted, becoming victims ourselves. Barging into a hostile or unstable environment for a primarily exploitive purpose is outright asking for trouble. The scenario had me asking myself quite often if I was selling out to a system that I didn't believe in. However, those doubts were overshadowed by the joy I got from doing feel-good feature stories and being able to rub elbows with the stars who were always shining in New York. But my celebrity encounters weren't always what I hoped for.

The day I heard Sylvester Stallone would be coming by, I almost dropped dead. His rags-to-riches Rocky story and, of course, his being a paisano, made the Italian Stallion my idol. I positioned myself outside the NBC makeup room, where he would go before heading into the studio. As he approached with an entourage, I couldn't believe how short he was: a mere 5'9" compared to my 6'5". I extended my hand, introduced myself and asked if I could get a quick picture with him.

He nodded, mumbled, "OK," and said nothing else during our brief encounter. Not that I was expecting him to yell out his trademark line from the movie – *Adrienne!* – But he certainly didn't live up to the larger-than-life image I had of him. In the picture, someone forgot to cue Mr. Stallone to smile for the camera.

Our 5 PM newscast, called *Live at 5*, brought in a daily array of celebrities to our Studio: 6 B, which was right across from the famous Studio 6 A, onetime home of Johnny Carson's Tonight Show and then the David Letterman Show, which began the year I started working at News 4 NY. It wasn't unusual for me to be standing at a urinal with Letterman at the latrine next to me, taking a last-minute leak before taping his show. One time, while we were both doing our business, he turned to me with his characteristic sarcasm and said, "Well, do you have any good murders that you'll be telling us about at 11 tonight?"

I was honored that NBC's new late night host knew who I was. Whenever I had a half hour or so before heading out to my story – perhaps a murder, like Letterman suggested – I'd sit in the back row of the audience and watch the 5:30 taping of *Late Night with David Letterman*. I also had inside access to watch broadcasts of *Saturday Night Live*, which was done up on the eighth floor on Studio 8 H. I could even wander into the backstage area and watch their rehearsals leading up to the show. 1983 was a rebuilding year for the show, following the departures of Chevy Chase, Dan Aykroyd, Gilda Radner and the tragic death of John Belushi.

Prior to the season premiere, I was told I was going to tape a preview feature that would air at the end of our Saturday 11 PM show leading into *SNL*. My crew and I shot some of the Saturday rehearsal and I was told I could interview the newest and youngest member of the upstart troupe: a twenty-one-year-old comic from Queens named Eddie Murphy. During our interview I found him to be poised, pleasant and honest, telling me that drugs and alcohol played no part in his personal life. He also concluded the interview by saying he had just been signed to do a movie which he believed was titled *Two Days*. That reference was to *48 Hours*, the detective comedy with Nick Nolte. The Box office smash catapulted Eddie's career to eventual superstardom.

Also located in the 30 Rock complexes were the second-floor studios of WNBC AM, the corporation's flagship radio station. Its personality-driven format was led by the original bad boy of the airwaves, Don Imus, who for years hosted the extremely popular *IMUS in the Morning* program. The same Imus who, you may recall, got fired from NBC a few years ago when he referred to the Rutgers women's basketball team as "a bunch of nappy-headed hoes."

Back in '83, when Imus and NBC radio were atop the ratings, the station announced it had hired another bad boy of radio who had developed quite a following in Washington D.C. The repeated station promos declared, "Get ready: the outrageous Howard Stern is coming to 66 NBC." I thought, *that can't be the same Howard Stern who had been a classmate and buddy of mine at Boston University's School of Public Communication.* I remembered how the tall, gangly kid from Long Island had gotten kicked off the campus station for his off-color comments on topics ranging from race to sex. And yet, sure enough, one week later I was heading down the hall to the NBC cafeteria when I ran smack-dab into my BU buddy, with whom I hadn't spoken since graduation seven years earlier. He told me that, after being fired from several radio stations, his act caught on in Washington D.C. a few years back. I purposely use the word "act" because Howard off-air is a shy, polite and personable guy. However, early on he realized that there was a market for outrageous radio disc jockeys, the ones who said the kind of politically incorrect things that many listeners assumed would never be said on public air waves. Stern said it always had been a childhood dream to come back to New York and work for the perennial powerhouse that was WNBC. He went on to tell me how exciting it was for him every time he saw me on NEWS 4 NY. I said it was quite a rush that both of us, just 30 years old, were at working at the number one media company in the number one market.

As we parted, Howard said that he wished he could enjoy his newfound fame, but added, "No matter how successful I get in this business, I will always remain paranoid, worrying it could all be snatched away from me in a second."

Being a reporter at a local TV station in New York meant often having to cover the national or international stories happening on Wall Street, Broadway or in the United Nations. I'll never forget the night I was assigned to cover an emergency session at the UN. They were addressing the crisis in the Falkland Islands. My producer Janet

Paist said I'd be doing a live report, the lead story at 11. She handed me some wire copy with background information on the unfolding crisis. Out the door I went, going into the news car with my crew and off we went to the world-famous house of diplomacy on Manhattan's east side. I couldn't help feeling overwhelmed as I walked into the auditorium where all the international representatives were engaged in discussion. I thought that, in most TV markets, a reporter would cover a city council meeting. Only in New York was the local correspondent expected to be an authority on international affairs, even if the story was only to fill the one minute forty-five seconds of allotted air time.

After my crew shot video of the proceedings, they went back outside to the live news truck which was parked about a block away from the UN building. I told them that, since I needed to get the latest update for our lead story, I'd stay in the auditorium and take notes before heading out to do my live report. There was only fifteen minutes to go before my live shot, yet the marathon session continued. I left the auditorium and headed for the elevator that would take me to the building's main level.

Once on the elevator, I began rehearsing my live report when, suddenly, the doors opened. I started walking down the darkened hall and realized I must have gotten off on the basement floor. I hurried back to the elevator and waited what seemed to be five minutes. No elevator. It was five to eleven, so I hightailed it up a stairwell, only to find the next level's exit door locked. I panicked and started pounding on the door. A security guard happened to be making his rounds right then and opened it for me. I went dashing toward the building exit, but knew I was still half a block away from my live shot location.

One minute to eleven and I saw my crew waving frantically at me.

30 seconds. My technician handed me my mike as I put in my earpiece. I hear: *The crisis in the Falklands is the topic of discussion tonight at the United Nations. News 4's Tony Pagnotti has been at the UN all night and has this live report.*

That's right, Chuck. Without missing a beat or as much as a gasping breath (think Asheville), I delivered my report with the authority and credibility of a well-versed international correspondent. *Live at the UN, I'm Tony Pagnotti, News 4, New York.*

Photographer Eric Kunkhe and sidekick Richie Tracks were laughing and shaking my hand, saying they thought I wasn't even going to make it in time for the spot, let alone pull it off so smoothly. Then it was time to unwind with a cold one or two at Hurley's bar, the official watering hole for the hardworking TV folks at 30 Rock.

Just a few doors down from Rockefeller Plaza, on the corner of 50th Street and Sixth Avenue, is Hurley's, affectionately referred to as Studio H. After the 6 and 11 PM newscasts the bar would be crammed three deep with anchors, reporters, photographers, editors, producers and all the rest of the people responsible for putting New York's top rated newscasts on the air. Libations and laughter were plentiful, especially when the dean of our reporting staff was holding court.

Bob Teague was a twenty-five-year veteran of WNBC and the first African-American reporter on a New York news program. A gifted storyteller, Bob turned his tales of the TV biz into a bestselling book called *Live and Off Color-the TV News Business*. With a background as a newspaper reporter, Bob said TV news was less about journalism and more about entertainment. He blamed news management, whom he referred to as "empty suits," for making local news a showcase for the sensational, silly and stupid.

From one of my own on-location experiences, I'd add "sometimes scary" to that list. Realizing that news crews get sent to some potentially unsafe locations, NBC management hired off-duty, plain-clothes NYPD officers to act as security. During many of our live shots, they were on the scene to protect the talent and crew, not to mention the expensive equipment that was needed to produce a live shot. But, sometimes, due to the nature of breaking news, a security officer couldn't get to a location in time.

That's what happened the time I was sent to be live on an underground train platform in lower Manhattan, where a minor equipment malfunction had caused a temporary shutdown of the system. As I got in place, my crew put up the portable TV monitor that allows a reporter to see the on-air picture being broadcast from the scene. That invariably draws large crowds of onlookers who know that, if they gather round the reporter, they have a chance of being on the news. Since I had no security officer to disperse them, I used a bit of psychology by saying they were all welcome to stand behind me, but not to wave and scream at the camera, or else the director would end the live shot and no one would get on TV.

Subway traffic in lower Manhattan is getting back to normal tonight after an equipment malfunction shut the L line down for a while, causing a big mess for straphangers. News 4 NY's Tony Pagnotti is live at the scene right now with the latest.

Tony.

Well, Chuck. Fortunately, there were no injuries in this mishap, which could have been much worse. We have some video we will show you of earlier when this happened...

At this point, the director rolls videotape shot earlier while I begin a live voice-over narration from what I see on my TV monitor. But, ten seconds into my narration, I felt a hand from behind me in the crowd reach into my back pants pocket where my wallet was.

I continued talking over the tape and, with one big swoop of my elbow, I swung around and grabbed my wallet. The would-be pickpocket scurried away and rushed up the subway steps. I finished my report and no one at home had any idea that this intrepid reporter singlehandedly took the law into his own hands while broadcasting.

The story got a lot of play at Hurley's. But Bob Teague came up to me and whispered "I'm not trying to steal your thunder, Tony, but I had a similar but even scarier thing happen to me at a subway derailment about five years ago. There was a big crowd of teenagers around me as I was narrating my video when, all of a sudden, I feel a hand reach up and grab my crotch for a few seconds. My voice may have gone up an octave or two for a few seconds but, like you, I just kept on talking."

Letting out a big laugh, I said, "Bob, only in New York does a reporter on location have to worry about protecting both his wallet and family jewels."

Bob and a few other veteran reporters were challenging management mandates to place reporters live on locations where, earlier in the day, spot news had happened, but by news time there was nothing to see. We heartily agreed with his cynicism of going live for the sake of going live. In his book, he minced no words when he wrote, "Silly Live Reports (SLR's) are the equivalent of jerking off in public." Not that I was ever a proponent of public indecency, but I must say I developed quite a reputation for pulling off some very good SLR's. I would never just stand there and deliver my report. I would look for opportunities to walk and talk the viewers through my live location, often using props to better illustrate my story. My stand-ups didn't sound stilted or memorized. My casual writing style resulted in a conversational delivery. There may have been thousands out there in TV land, but I always like to think I was communicating with one person.

My favorite "lives" were those famous New York show biz parties, like the one I did at the world famous *Studio 54* for the opening of *Conan the Barbarian*. I couldn't believe it. There I was, smack in the middle of the deafening revelry, eye-to-eye on live TV with Arnold Schwartzenegger, asking him about his Herculean starring role.

Whether I was covering a star-studded movie or a theater premiere, a murder in Manhattan or a fatal fire in Flatbush, the NBC brass was impressed with my versatility.

The ultimate compliment came when Jack Phillips stopped me in the hall and said with a smile, "I thought you might be interested in knowing that Connie Collins decided to return from maternity leave and come back to work. But we would still like to offer you a full-time position."

I shook his hand and blurted out, "Fantastic!"

"Have your agent call me so we can see about getting you a contract."

"Sure, will do," I agreed, not letting on that I didn't have an agent and wondering if I really needed one. I quickly got the answer to that question when I started talking to my newsroom colleagues. Every reporter and anchor had a high-powered agent who got paid anywhere from two to ten percent of the client's annual salary.

When I indicated to Bob Teague that I could save that yearly fee by doing my own deal, he shook his head, put his hand on my shoulder and said, "Pag, you're in the big leagues now, and these managers play hardball when it comes to contract talks."

"But Phillips tells me how much he likes my work, so why wouldn't he want to offer me a fair contract"?

"My friend, there's an old saying in this business: 'we love you, we love you, we love you, you're fired.' Management likes to use negotiations to play games when it comes down to talking turkey. That's why most agents shop around to see what other stations might be interested in their clients' services. That gives the agent more bargaining power when the suits come in with a lowball offer to try and seal the deal." Those words of wisdom prompted me to sign with N.S. Beinstock, a top-notch agency which, in addition to representing a number of other New York talent, boasted a stable of network stars including Dan Rather and Mike Wallace.

Feeling good about the prospects of becoming a fully-fledged member of the WNBC 4 news team, I realized that I would soon have to consider alternatives to what had become a grueling daily commute to and from my home in New Haven. There were times after finishing my 11 PM news report when I would have to dash to Grand Central and jump on the last train out. And, when a live shot location was too far for me to catch the midnight train to New Haven, the station would put me up for the night at the Hyatt near 30 Rock. When I got home, I'd go to bed and before I knew it, it was time to get up and catch the noon train back to Gotham City.

It wouldn't be fair to ask Barbara to move to New York, since she had a job she loved and some good friends in New Haven. We wound up compromising by buying a condo in Stamford, Connecticut, which was a forty-five-minute train ride to Grand Central. As part of our compromise, I agreed with my wife that we would see if a therapist might help us strengthen what was a longtime shaky marriage.

The nomadic lifestyle and unpredictable firings were undoubtedly contributing factors to there being such a high divorce rate in TV. In my many heart-to-heart talks with my colleagues at Hurley's, I heard more than once that a hard-driving commitment to building up a TV career is directly proportional to the breaking up of a relationship or marriage.

When it came to ratings, NEWS 4 NEW YORK was at the top of the heap, led by our dynamic anchor team of Chuck Scarborough and Sue Simmons. A very well respected, award winning newsman and author Chuck was believed to someday be the heir apparent to the NBC Network anchorman position, succeeding Tom Brokaw. Sue, a beautiful African-American woman with Lena Horne looks and her engaging personality, was made for television, earning quite a following of loyal viewers. Around the newsroom and on the news set, she was always joking and loved to talk about whatever was on her mind.

One time, Simmons made an infamous on-air blooper that was heard round the cyberspace world. She and co-anchor Chuck Scarborough were getting ready to do a tease which ran a half hour prior the 11 PM newscast. Ninety percent of the time those pre-show updates are taped and can be redone if an anchor messes up while reading the prompter. Apparently, someone didn't remind Sue that this tease wasn't being recorded and was going out live. *"Good evening. I'm Sue Simmons and I'm Chuck Scarborough, coming up on News 4, tonight at 11.* Somehow, Chuck didn't realize he was scripted to read the first part of the tease and just looked into the camera saying nothing. Which prompted Sue to swear, "What the fuck are you doing?"

Fade to Black. Back to Programming. The NBC switchboards lit up with viewers saying they couldn't believe what they heard Sweet Sue say. All the newspapers ran stories on the blooper heard round the Big Apple and wondered whether the 30 Rock brass would discipline or fire the grand dame of WNBC. But they did neither. The next night, the very embarrassed anchorwoman apologized for the "foul language she regrettably used on the air," and said that she would not let it happen ever again. Apparently, the veteran anchor had never heard the number one rule of broadcasting: whenever wearing a microphone, behave like it's turned on and everything being said is being broadcast to the masses.

My agent, Carole Cooper, called to tell me that Jack Phillips and the station attorney were not exactly showing their love for Tony Pagnotti by what they were offering in dollars and cents. Even though they were offering me a three-year contract, the salary increases amounted to only about three thousand dollars each year. Doing the math, those increases would barely cover my six percent yearly agent's fee. Carol told me that we could walk away from their offer and pursue a station in Los Angeles that expressed an interest in me. But, considering I just bought a condo in Connecticut, I wasn't going to even entertain that possibility. I told Carol that even though I was disappointed in the money being offered, I was pleased I had job security for three years and would sign on the dotted line.

The ink wasn't even dry on my contract when Jack Phillips called me in his office and asked, "Have you ever done weather before?"

"No, why?"

"Well, the station's longtime legendary weatherman, Dr. Frank Field, has lots of vacation time coming up and his backup just left for job in LA."

"You mean, you want me to do the weather?"

"Sure, you have the personality, and you do great live shots."

"Yeah, but I don't know anything about meteorology."

"That's ok; there's a staff meteorologist who prepares the forecast and the green screen graphics for you. TV weather is ninety percent performance, ten percent information. So, how would you like to fill in next week for a few days?"

As much as I wanted to say, "No, thanks," I blurted out, "Ok, I'll try it." After cramming some background weather info from meteorology texts, I practiced in front of the studio green screen. At first it was so disorientating, pointing at maps behind me that weren't really there. Images were electronically superimposed and the trick was to look at TV monitors situated just outside of camera range to ensure that I knew I was positioned just right. Being off in my gesticulations just a bit meant the difference of pointing to Nebraska instead of New York. So, there I was, standing in front of the big blank, green screen, moments away from my debut of doing weather in, of all places, the biggest TV market in the country. As I waited my turn, I began thinking of what would happen if my first forecast flopped. It would be all over the tabloids in the morning; I could see the entertainment headline in the *New York Post:* DARK CLOUDS HANG OVER WEATHERMAN'S STORMY START.

Anchor weather intro; *Well, Tony Pagnotti is in today over in the weather center, filling in for Dr. Frank. So, Tony, will we need our umbrellas tomorrow?*

Tony, ad lib: *Well, Sue, if you let your smile be your umbrella tomorrow, you'll get a mouth full of rain.*

And with that corny ad lib, a weatherman was born. I felt poised and in control as I precisely pointed to the highs and lows on the map, breezing through my three-minute segment. Afterwards, I got a lot of "attaboys" in the newsroom, including accolades from my boss who said I looked like I'd been doing weather for years. I felt this could be the start of something big, especially since weatherman are right up there with the anchor people in pay and star power. But that dream would have to be on hold, since I knew I was only a fill-in forecaster who would continue to grind out the day-to-day general assignment stories and live shots. There were times I would be doing a live shot of a subway train derailment at 6 PM and then would be needed back in the studio to be the personable prognosticator for News 4 NY at 11.

One night when I got back to the station after covering a murder, Dr. Frank stopped me in the hall and told me he'd heard through the corporate grapevine that the station might be hiring a full-time forecaster in the next few months, and that he would be my "rabbi" in backing me for the position. I thanked him for the scoop and support and walked away smiling, thinking how, if that ever happened, I would be sitting on top of the TV world. Not only would my star rise significantly, but my salary would probably reach a meteoric $200,000. There, too, would be a big personal payoff, going from reporter to weatherman. I would never again have to stick a microphone in front of grieving people and ask the insidious, HOW DO YOU FEEL?

In addition to my day-to-day reporting, I was called upon on the average of about once a week to be a fill-in forecaster. One of my most memorable appearances in front of the green screen came during the Christmas holiday season. As you probably know, Rockefeller Plaza is lit up with a giant Christmas tree that attracts thousands of visitors every day. The joy the seasonal sight brings to the world is a pain in the jingle bells for those who work inside 30 Rockefeller Center. The area around the tree and skating rink is gridlocked from both vehicle and pedestrian traffic, making it a daunting task to navigate through the crowds and get to the building's entrance.

But once the NBC employees made it into work, they sure knew how to get into the holiday spirit. Starting in the first week of December and leading up to Christmas Eve, the more than 50 company departments took turns hosting parties on their respective floors. Regardless if an NBC employee worked for WNBC-TV, radio, Network News, The Today Show, or David Letterman, everyone was invited to bounce from party to party where booze and food were plentiful.

It was a few nights before Christmas and I was scheduled to do the 11 PM weather. With that in mind, I promised myself I would limit my intake of holiday libations to just one or two. I kept that promise for the first party I hit. Then, it was on to the next celebration, where I met up with Don Pardo, the longtime booming voice of Saturday Night Live. As I discovered, the 75-year-old announcer sure liked his vodka and tonic. And so did I. We decided to party hop together and that one cocktail led to another, and another and before I knew it, I was feeling a wee bit tipsy with show time about an hour away.

I headed down to studio 6B where all my weather graphics were assembled and ready to go. All I had to do was go out there and make sure that, while delivering the weather, I didn't fall overboard into the ocean on my weather maps. Physically, I felt fine, but I was wondering if my holiday buzz might be noticeable on the air. I took my seat on the set next to our nationally-known sports anchor Marv Albert. During the commercial I tried not to chat too much with Marv, wondering if he might detect the alcohol on my breath.

Anchor intro: *Let's check in with Tony and see if we might be in for a white Christmas. Tony...*

With that, it was like a racehorse firing out of the starting gate. I felt like I was uncontrollably sprinting through my forecast but never slurred or stumbled over a word. It seemed like my three minutes were over in 30 seconds. The anchors thanked me and, as the commercial break began, Marv turned to me and with his notorious play by play voice said very sincerely, "Tony that was one of the smoothest flowing forecasts I have ever seen. Nice job." I thought, *YES!, I'll drink to that.*

Even though the relocation to Stamford cut my New Haven commute in half, I still found myself missing more and more of the last midnight trains out of Grand Central. Often, I missed the connection because my crew and I were stuck somewhere in traffic on our way back to the studio from an 11 PM live shot. But, I must admit, there were those times when I could have made it to the train station on time but instead opted to hang out with my cronies at Hurley's. This pattern, of course, did nothing to help strengthen my already shaky marriage. When my wife and I met with a marriage counselor he concluded that spending more time at work than at home would lead nowhere but to divorce court. He suggested I talk to my boss about changing my schedule in order to have a few nights off. When I did just that, my boss advised me that that was not the way TV works, and I would have to make a choice of being married to my job or to Barbara. Inwardly, I knew what my decision would have to be.

Despite the obligatory daily diet of death and destruction I had to dish out in my reports, what really made me tick were those "Only in New York" feature stories and occasional weather appearances. I knew with a little patience and blessing from my Rabbi Dr. Frank, it would be just a matter of time before my career would be launched up into the stratosphere. But then, like most things in life, unscripted twists and turns often come.

I had no sooner gotten back to my desk after a 6 PM live shot when the newsroom secretary, a sad look on her face, told me that Phillips wanted to see me in his office. From her look, I perceived that I wasn't being summoned to be told how I was being named WNBC's newest weatherman. "Things are always changing in this business," he began with a hushed voice, having difficulty making eye contact. "I've been asked by the GM to step down as news director and in the interim," he continued, "the folks upstairs are making some staff changes."

"So, are you telling me that I won't be moving into the weather slot?"

"Not only that, NBC corporate has mandated us to trim our budget, and you, being the last reporter hired, will have to be the first to go".

"But you have to honor the remainder of my three-year contract."

"Only for six more months. There's a window in the contract that gives us the option to terminate the existing time left."

With those words the dream of my career heading toward the stratosphere suddenly came crashing back down to earth. "But what about the weather job?" I asked. "That has to be filled. If not me, then who?"

"Our corporate consultants are hot on an up-and-coming personable weathercaster who has made a name for himself on Cleveland TV. I've seen his work and he reminds me of a black Willard Scott."

I didn't know whether to scream or cry, so I just stood up and headed toward the door. My world was about to be turned upside down by a Hurricane named Al Roker. Great move up for Al as you probably know went on to be the iconic TODAY SHOW weatherman. As word got out about my imminent departure, a number of my colleagues came up to me to express their shock and consolation. The general consensus was "how could a guy who is able to do it all, and do it very well, be sent packing?" My response was to quote the very knowledgeable Bob Teague: "We love you, we love you, we love you, you're fired."

My agent predictably stated that it was NBC's loss and that she would see if there might be any opportunities at the other stations in town. Meanwhile, back on the home front, Barbara and I agreed that things were never going to improve in our seven-year marriage. We would file for divorce and sell the Stamford condo. In the few months I had left before my last day on the job, I had the feeling of a man facing his date of execution. After a taste of the Big Apple, thoughts of going to any other city for work left a bitter taste in my mouth.

My friend and field producer Glen Barbour threw a big time farewell bash at a disco club on the Upper East Side. The next day in the *NY Post*, there was a picture of my colleagues toasting my good luck, along with an article saying that New York's Italian TV stallion Tony Pagnotti would be leaving WNBC. It didn't say why I was leaving or where I would be going, something I didn't even know myself.

7

SUDDENLY SINGLE, UNEMPLOYED AND LOOKING FOR A PLACE TO CALL HOME

After a fifteen-minute appearance in divorce court on July 26, 1984, my seven-year marriage was dissolved due to "irreconcilable differences." Barbara and I wished each other well and said we would keep in touch, but we never did. I got in my, car packed with clothes, a TV set and a microwave oven, and began heading toward the George Washington Bridge. As I crossed the giant span, I could see twilight descending on the city that never sleeps, and I wondered where I would now be sleeping. I pulled off the Jersey turnpike to a rest stop and called my sister. Ann Marie, who has always been there for her little brother, invited me to come to her apartment in Scranton to spend the night. I told her I was embarrassed to tell our parents that I was out of work with no place to call home. She assured me they would welcome me into their home with open arms.

Swallowing my pride, I moved back into the home I had departed seven years earlier to begin my journey into TV. It didn't take long for me to get used to my parents' hospitality. Home cooked Italian meals and Mom doing my laundry provided the TLC I needed. I knew this lifestyle couldn't last forever, but I was surely going to enjoy it. It also gave me a chance to reconnect with my parents whom I had seldom seen while living and working in four different states.

My agent would call me and tell me of stations in places like Denver, Miami, or Minneapolis that liked my tapes and were interested in interviewing me for reporter openings. I told her I wasn't interested in pursuing these positions since my days of general assignment reporting were over, and all I would consider now was a weather gig in a top 20 market. Since those openings seemed to be few, she kept saying that I needed to go on some of these interviews, if for nothing else than to get out of the cocoon that I had come to settle into at my folk's home. Carole finally convinced me to accept an invitation to discuss a reporter/anchor position for WMAR TV 2 in Baltimore. I heard Baltimore had really turned into quite a beautiful waterfront city since I last visited there as a boy to visit my Uncle Dan. What the heck. Since the station was paying for my airfare, hotel and meals, I'd go.

As it turned out, the News director and I had something in common. Ed Pruitt had been the news director at WLOS Asheville for a few years prior to my arrival in

1976. We immediately hit it off, exchanging stories about a lot of the same people we had worked with at Channel 13. With all the good-natured banter, both of us lost sight of the fact that I was in his office for a job interview. After he briefly explained the reporter/anchor position that was open, I politely told him that it didn't sound like a good career move for me at this time. Appreciating my honesty, Ed said he still wanted to take me to dinner before I headed back to the hotel.

So off we went to the Inner harbor, to a fine Italian restaurant where several rounds of Jack Daniels served as our appetizers. After dinner, with both of us feeling no pain, he drove us up I-83 to a dance club called Christopher's. There we downed some more Jack and soon two ladies came over and pulled us up on the dance floor. When the clock struck 2 AM the bar closed down and my partying buddy and I headed to the parking lot. When we arrived at the Cross Keys Hotel, I asked Ed if he was ok to drive to his home which was 45 minutes outside Baltimore. He said he didn't want to take the risk of getting pulled over and hit with a DUI. To which I suggested, "Since Channel 2 was paying for my room anyway, and it's got double beds, why not sleep it off here?"

When we got to the room, he called his wife. From the look on his face, she didn't believe his story that it was merely a case of a job interview that turned into an unexpected social direction. So, I got on the phone myself and tried to calm Mrs. Pruitt down, but she promptly hung up. Both of us hit our respective beds. Around 7 AM I heard Ed's alarm go off. He jumped out of bed and put back on his suit that had been draped over a desk chair. From my bed, I looked up at him with one eye closed. We both giggled and shook hands. As he left, I thought, *Oh well, I'll never be seeing him again.* Or so I thought.

As fate would have it, two weeks later my agent Carole called and said I had just gotten a call from the GM at TV 2 in Baltimore.

"They have a weekend weather position open and saw your weather demo and loved it."

"But when I was there Ed never said anything."

"That's because they had no idea you did weather in New York until they saw your forecasting tape. Since you already were interviewed, they said that, if you're interested, I can do the contract with them over the phone."

Within a few days the deal was done and I would be soon being starting a new job in Baltimore. I got a call from Ed congratulating me and saying how much he looked forward to me joining his team. Before hanging up, he said, "Would you mind keeping our shenanigans from a few weeks ago to ourselves?"

"Sure," I replied, "but someday, Ed, when I write my tell-all memoir, one chapter headline shall read:

8

I HAD TO SLEEP WITH THE BOSS TO GET MY JOB IN BALTIMORE.

So, after a six month hiatus from the business, I began the new year of 1985 packing a few suitcases along with my TV and stereo system and headed south down I-81 toward Baltimore. Even though I would be making less money than when I left New York, I felt like I had gotten a huge raise when I'd factored in the cheaper cost of living. My comfortable Roland Park apartment with all the amenities was only 400 bucks a month. In the Big Apple, the same place would rent for triple that figure.

When I pulled up to Channel 2, located just over the county line, I was amazed at the free, huge employee parking lot. No more paying top-dollar at restaurants, bars, and stores. In my contract, it stipulated that I would be the weekend weatherman and, on the other three days of the week, a reporter. But I told Carole Cooper that I wanted it stated somewhere in the agreement that I would do only feature stories or weather-related segments, with no general assignments unless it was an emergency. That was important to me, knowing that my days of covering death and destruction were over.

My first day on the job, January 28, 1985, saw a nasty ice and snow mix falling in Charm city. The producer asked me if I would like to get right into the thick of things by doing a live shot out on the messy Beltway during the 5 PM broadcast. A cab took me to the location where one cameraman, not a two-man crew like in New York, was waiting with his live truck and camera set up. As I approached him, there was a wry smile on what was to me a very familiar face.

"Remember me? Keith Fox?"

Oh my gosh, a flashback to about ten years earlier. Keith, who, at the time, was a senior in high school in Asheville, NC, was a part-time film editor at Channel 13 while I was working there. The one-time skinny teenager, was now grown-up, with a wife and two kids. He told me that Ed Pruitt, whom he worked for in Asheville, had brought him to Baltimore five years earlier.

"He didn't take you to Christopher's, did he?"

"Huh, what do you mean?"

"Never mind. We've got my first Baltimore live shot to do."

Good evening everyone I'm Ken Matz and I'm Sally Thorner: Our big story tonight, the wrath of Mother Nature. A mix of snow and ice has been falling around Baltimore, causing some real slow-going on the roads. Let's get the latest from the newest member of the News Scene Two family: Tony Pagnotti. Welcome, Tony. Wish we had better weather to greet you with.

Thanks, Ken and Sally. The ice man cometh to the beltway here at Charles Street where traffic right now is slip-sliding away

It didn't take me long to see how snow-phobic Baltimore was. The standing joke was that as soon as there were predictions of the white stuff, folks would go scurrying to the store and buy toilet paper, bread and milk. The rationale was that, if by chance you became snowbound in your home for several days, those were the mandatory items you needed in a survival kit. We, the media just fed the frenzied thinking by warning:

THINGS ARE A MESS OUT THERE. DON'T DRIVE UNLESS YOU REALLY HAVE TO. BE SURE TO ALLOW PLENTY OF EXTRA TIME. BLOWING AND DRIFTING CAN CAUSE WHITEOUT CONDITONS AND RESULT IN ZERO VISIBILTY.

The Channel 2 two slogan regularly being promoted on commercials and billboards was: "*We're friends you can turn 2.*" To which one could add, "Especially when it comes to scaring the crap out of you."

In a way, I felt like a born-again broadcaster in my transition from New York to Baltimore. Being the big fish in a smaller pond was working out swimmingly. I felt the only way to be accepted as the new TV guy in town was to be seen in the community among the viewers. So, every Saturday and Sunday, a few hours prior to the 6 PM news, I'd go out with a photographer to cover the big festival, fair, parade, etc., have some fun on camera with the people and then introduce the tapes from the studio after completing my weather report.

When I wasn't reporting on outdoor events, I would find feel-good human interest stories to attend, such as birthday parties for 100-year-olds or perhaps a high school dance marathon to raise money for a charitable cause. I quickly found out how big-hearted Baltimore was when it came to reaching out to organizations and individuals in need. I was often asked to be an MC or honorary chairman for various fundraising functions. In addition to being a part of the festivities, prior to the event I would use some of my time at the weather map to plug and promote. "Hey, next Sunday head to the Inner Harbor and cheer me on in the annual Crab Picking contest to benefit our young friends at the Johns Hopkins Children's center."

Raising money and awareness for worthy community causes was something that TV needed to do more. After all, the origins of broadcasting were built on the premise that "the airwaves belong to the people" and that, when granted a license, a station took on the pledge of serving the public interest. I was fortunate because my bosses at Channel 2 gave me *carte blanche* when it came to putting in as much time and effort into community involvement as I desired. In many cases, my involvement went beyond my role as a broadcaster. One Sunday, I got a frantic call from our station's promotion director that one of our news anchors was ill but, in a few hours, he was supposed to MC a Walk for Cystic Fibrosis. She asked if I could pinch hit.

"Sure, I'll make it my weather feature for tonight." As I walked toward the colorfully-decorated high school field, adorned with banners proclaiming *Fight Cystic Fibrosis and Walk for Breath*, I thought how, even though it was a last minute request, I wished I had the chance to find out just what "cystic fibrosis" was.

It didn't take long for me to get my answer. No sooner had the PR woman handed me a script of the day's festivities, than she said, "I'd like for you to meet our Walk for Breath youth ambassador, Brian Gray.

Sitting in a wheelchair with oxygen tubes attached to his nostrils was a handsome, but frail, blond-haired, blue-eyed boy. His handshake was firm, despite the feel of very boney fingers. With a smile, he thanked me for filling in on a moment's notice. He told me not to worry about not knowing anything about CF, explaining he would take care of that once I introduced him. Boy, did he! The twelve-year-old addressed the crowd with credibility and confidence. He told a hushed audience that the average life expectancy of a child with the incurable genetic respiratory disease was fourteen. It was at that age that his older brother, Sean, who also had CF, had died. Even though Brian knew that a cure for the disease would not help to save his life, he talked selflessly of how babies currently being diagnosed could possibly go on to live normal lives. From our first meeting, that courageous young man and I became fast friends for what turned out to sadly be much too short a time.

After less than six months in Charm City, I seemed to be developing a following among viewers. Two bits of shtick I used every week during my weather were especially popular. I began each segment by holding up two fingers and saying, "Baltimore, let's go out the door and check our weather twooooo-gether." Then, after giving the temperature, I'd purposely refer to the moisture percentage in the air as the *"HUM-A DIT-ITY."* Whether I was in the grocery store or the dentist's office, it was common for folks to come up to me and recite what became a Baltimore catchphrase.

But not everyone was a big fan of my whimsical weather. I had just walked back into the newsroom from the studio when a producer said there was an irate caller on the phone who wanted to speak to Mr. Pagnotti's supervisor. "Sure," I said, "Transfer the call to me".

"Hi. This is Mr. Pagnotti's supervisor. How may I help you?"

"Well, let me tell you something," began the high-pitched, elderly woman's voice. "I am a retired Baltimore English teacher and I do not like how, every time Mr. Pagnotti is on TV, he mispronounces the word 'humidity'. It sets a bad example for children watching the weather."

"Ma'am, you know, you're right. I had never thought about the impact his improper use of language might have on Baltimore's youth, so I am going to terminate Mr. Pagnotti immediately."

After a five second silence, the caller said, "Well... That action is perhaps a bit severe. He should be reprimanded."

"Oh no, ma'am, I am so glad you called, and I am going to fire him right now."

When I hung up, my newsroom colleagues were all laughing and shaking their heads.

I actually had been reprimanded from time to time for saying "hum-a-did-ity" from my boss, Ed. Because of the audience following I had built up in such a short time, he avoided messing with my shtick, but he made no bones about how much he hated hearing it on air. One night, after coming back to the weather office following a dinner break, there was a handwritten note on my desk. On stationery with the banner *FROM THE DESK OF ED PRUITT* was written: *Tony, this is your last warning. You used that stupid word on the 6 PM weather. I better not hear it at 11, or else. Signed, ED P.*

I walked out into the newsroom and asked where Ed was. Sports director Scott Garceau said he had gone home for the night shortly after he went out of the weather office. Enraged, I said, "Well, he left me a note indicating that I'd be fired if I said hum-a-did-ity tonight at 11. So, I am going to call him at home now and say if that's all it takes to fire me, then I'll save him the trouble and resign."

As I started dialing the phone, Scott came over and, laughing, took the phone and hung it up. "What are you doing?"

"I'm serious."

"Well, I didn't know you would get so bent so out of shape, or I wouldn't have written that phony note on that Pruitt stationary pad I found in his office."

It was a prank that almost had me calling in my resignation to the boss at home.

9

CUPID'S ARROW FOLLOWS THE JETSTREAM TO A WEATHERMAN'S HEART

Before long, I became the Channel 2 good-will ambassador of the airwaves. Whether I was championing the cause of the Johns Hopkins Children's Center or participating in the various ethnic festivals around town, I began earning a reputation as Charm City's number one cheerleader. My promotional work did not go unnoticed by Baltimore's number one citizen: Mayor William Donald Schaefer, who has been singlehandedly credited with turning Baltimore into a world-class renaissance city. Schaefer became famous nationwide for promoting his city with outlandish stunts, such as when he dove into the tanks of the newly-built national aquarium with an old-fashioned bathing suit and rubber ducky. The first time I met him was at press event promoting a city fundraising event: Fill a pothole for your sweetie on Valentine's Day. With camera rolling, I invited his honor to join me in a chorus of *LET ME CALL YOU SWEETHEART I FILLED A POTHOLE FOR YOU.* The exclusive duet was a hit on our 6 PM news and the talk of the town. That was the start of a nice promotional partnership and friendship with Schaefer. Little did I know that the mayor would also be instrumental in helping lead me to another relationship in which I would one day be exchanging "I do's."

Coming to Baltimore not only meant not only starting a new career but also beginning a new life as a single man. Since I had been engaged or married to Barbara for most of my adult life, I wanted to make up for all those years of lost dating. Being a new guy on TV in a new town certainly helped to boost one's bachelorhood stock. I found myself taking advantage of my newfound freedom and fame by being quite the cavorting Don Juan around town. I promised myself I would never get married again, and casual relationships would suffice.

On a September night in 1985, with that frame of mind and a few vodka tonics under my belt, I was at a media party for a new establishment downtown – Billy's Bar and Restaurant. Free food and booze were plentiful at these events. And when everything's on the house, you can expect a ton of TV people to be in attendance. As the night wore on, I began scanning the crowd for young ladies that might catch my eye. I spotted a blonde-haired, blue-eyed girl who I hadn't seen at any other media parties. We struck up a conversation. She told me her name was Sandy. She was at the party as a representative from Mayor Schaefer's promotional office, called *Baltimore's Best*. Her duty was to present the new restaurant owner with an official mayoral proclamation declaring that day "Billy's Bar and Restaurant Day in Baltimore."

After some cordial chit chat, I cut to the chase and asked if she'd like to leave Billy's and join me for more drinks at Christopher's, the same bar that Ed Pruitt took me to conclude my intoxicating interview. Perhaps sensing that I appeared to be a smooth operator, or maybe it was because I was a few sheets to the wind, she declined my offer and also refused to give me her phone number. So, I left Billy's alone, decided not to go to Christopher's and instead headed home alone.

The next day I was determined to find out more about that pretty lady from the mayor's office who had the nerve to deflect the advances of Mr. TV 2 himself. After a few well-placed calls, I found that her name was Sandy Sneen, and she had recently been hired by the *Baltimore's Best* office after serving as an intern for the office right out of college, in 1985. That made her all of twenty-two ten years old, ten years younger than me. But what did that matter; it wasn't like I was looking to marry her. The next time I saw the mayor out at an event, I told him about my chance meeting with Sandy and asked if he would tell her what a good guy I was.

During my first year at WMAR, the perennially third-rated station in town was starting to make some upward movement in the ratings. Just prior to my hiring, the station had brought in good looking co-anchors Ken Matz and

Sally Thorner. Matz was a handsome, square-jawed veteran newsman from Philadelphia. Thorner was an up-and-coming, bubbly brunette who one consultant observed had the uncanny ability to deliver each news story "as if she were making love to the camera."

I believe that the most popular anchors are those who are perceived by the audience to be the most sincere which, in some cases, just means being a good performer. Studio crew members would often tell stories of how one certain anchorwoman would introduce a reporter's taped story about a tragic accident or murder with a deeply pained and saddened look. Then, right after that tape started playing, she would pick up the phone and call Nordstrom's to see if the shoes she had ordered had come in. The floor director would tell her five seconds back to the studio live. At the last second, the acting anchor would hang up the phone and be cued to let her know she was live on camera one. Then, looking like she had just lost her best friend, the anchorwoman would shake her head, commenting: "Such a sad story."

While TV news has earned a reputation as often being insensitive and shallow, I believe that, when used properly, there is no other medium that has such an emotional and intimate impact. Through the marriage of words and pictures, the broadcast journalist is able to communicate very personal stories to the viewing public. It was that type of human interest story that I was doing on a regular basis on Channel 2. I would often get letters and calls from viewers letting me know about a person, place or subject that was my kind of story. My most memorable feature stories during my thirty-four years in TV did not originate from press releases or the assignment editor, but instead came from the viewers themselves. And, every now and then, one of those viewers showed up at my door.

The station receptionist called my desk to tell me a Mr. Polk was in the lobby and would like to see me, so that he could tell me about his son. Even though I was in the middle of writing my story for the 5 PM news, I thought any guy who randomly shows up at a TV station to talk to a reporter must have a pretty interesting child.

He began, "I appreciate your coming out to see me, I know you must be busy but I'll make this quick. I have a seven-year-old son named Chris who is your biggest fan, he thinks you're a cool dude and loves it when you say 'hum-adidity' on the weather."

"That's so nice, I appreciate you coming by to tell me. Maybe someday I'll get a chance to meet him."

Without missing a beat he responded, "Well, how about three weeks from this Saturday night, at the Arbutus VFW hall? You see, Chris has been battling cancer for two years now and folks in our community have been nice enough to throw a fundraising bull roast in honor of Chris, to help my family with some of our medical costs."

"Well, I'd love to, but, as you know, I do weekend weather."

"Oh, that's right. Well, I appreciate your time anyway".

But as turned to leave, I said, "But maybe I can run down to the hall for an hour during my dinner break."

"That would be fantastic."

Not only did I make it to the bull roast that night, I took along a photographer to video some of the festivities which I would run after my weather report at 11. The first person to greet us as we entered the hall was a spunky, bald-headed boy with a big smile who slapped me a high five and said, "Hey, Tony, how's the ole humadidity out there tonight?" Other than having no hair, you would never have suspected that Chris was waging a battle against a deadly disease. I was so impressed with his courageous spirit that I did a follow-up story a few weeks later on him being his little league team's third baseman. Just like with Brian Gray, I became friends with the Polks, and was even invited to family functions like birthdays and anniversaries.

My human interest stories usually aired as the last segment of our five o'clock news, which led into the 6 PM news. There is a tried and true formula in the TV news business that, no matter how dire or depressing the first 57 minutes of a news program might be, in the last few minutes you need to leave the viewer with a smile by running a feel-good, warm and fuzzy, or even funny, feature story. Since my stories fell into one of these categories, one of our news managers suggested we give a franchise name to my show-enders. Some names were tossed out, like *Pag's people*, or *Tony's Good News*. But in the end, management decided on "Tony's Travels." In the station on-air promotions, viewers were invited each night to go along for the ride with *Tony's Travels*. In addition to on-air promotions and newspaper ads, the station had powder blue T-shirts made with a large caricature of me sitting in a tiny sports car that bore the TV news station logo. As much as I was flattered to be depicted on a T-shirt, I felt a little awkward when I was told to give away the T-shirts on camera to folks. Nothing like a little shameless self-promotion.

During the first several months in Charm City, my carefree bachelor lifestyle found me going out on occasional dates but never more than once with the same girl. It was all a part of my promise to steer clear of serious relationships. But promises are made to be broken, and that's what happened as I began seeing twenty-two-year-old Sandy Sneen of *Baltimore's Best* fame on a weekly basis. She told me that one of the reasons she decided to go out with me was because her boss Mayor Schaefer stopped by her desk and told her to "give that big Italian guy on TV a break." How cool was that? The Mayor of Baltimore thought enough of me to play cupid .The decade age difference between us didn't seem to matter. We would usually meet up for dinner every weekend during my breaks between the 6 and 11 newscasts. My previous cavorting around bars and clubs in Baltimore came to a halt as I spent more and more time one-on-one with Sandy.

10

TONY'S TRAVELS GOES INTERNATIONAL

Most of the *Tony's Travels* stories were done with Electronic News Gathering (ENG) microwave vans or with the station's huge satellite truck, a big red 2 showing on the side. My destinations were generally confined to "slice of life" stories within Maryland and D.C. However, occasionally, I travelled to some cool faraway places. When the *Make A Wish* foundation for seriously ill children decided to send my buddy Brian Gray to Disneyworld, I got to tag along and capture some very magical moments for the viewers back in Baltimore. It was also in Disneyworld where I participated in Goofy Games. The shrewd PR folks at Disney came up with the annual event where talent from TV stations around the country were invited, along with contest winners from their respective cities, to take part in three days of competitive, fun-filled games set up throughout the park. Events ranged from racing down water slides to relay races on the Disney beaches. Disney paid for the all the participants' airfare, food and lodging. In return, about thirty reporters from around the country beamed reports back to their hometown station every night, which, of course, had Mickey Mouse smiling from ear to ear.

The promise of TV coverage really helped to get me into places that would normally not have been accessible to me. I had done a few stories on a blind Baltimore woman who sang country music at some area clubs. The mother of five told me her dream was to visit Nashville someday. So, I picked up the phone and called the folks at the Grand Ole Opry and asked if they could arrange for us to tour backstage. They loved the idea and, before you knew it, Peggy and I were on a plane, headed to Nashville. With me guiding her from dressing room to dressing room, Peggy was in seventh heaven as she chatted with some very friendly and accommodating country stars like Roy Clarke, Grandpa Jones, Loretta Lynn and one handsome young man making his Opry debut that night: Alan Jackson.

Local TV coverage can even have clout internationally. Mike Polk called me one night at home and said that, recently, coming home from Chris's chemo treatment at the Johns Hopkins Children's center, his son had asked, "Dad, do kids in other countries get cancer?"

Mike said he explained to Chris that, unfortunately, the disease attacks kids from all over the world.

To which his son replied, "Gee, someday I'd like to meet some of them and tell them to keep fighting, like me, and then they'll be all right."

Mike said he told that story in a letter he'd sent to a US representative he knew at the embassy in Switzerland.

"Now, here's the good news," Mike continued, "I got a phone call this morning from the embassy and was told that they could arrange for Chris to visit with cancer patients at a local hospital in Zurich." Better yet, the embassy rep told Mike that he could probably get airfare donated for Mike, his wife and Chris to fly from Baltimore to Switzerland.

"Fantastic, Mike. What a trip."

"Yes, and I was thinking what a great *Tony's Travels* story it would make."

"It would be awesome, Mike. But I've got to tell you, the station will never pay the Swiss airfare and lodging for both myself and a cameraman. However, it can't hurt to ask." The next day I went into Ed's office, already knowing what his response would be. He rolled his eyes, saying he could never justify spending around 3,000 dollars for me to go. But, an hour later, I was at my desk when Ed, along with the station GM, Art Simon, walked up to me, wearing big smiles.

"Why the shit-eating grins?" I asked.

"Oh, nothing," said Art, "we're just happy that we'll be rid of you, that week you'll be in Switzerland."

I couldn't believe it. Art said he thought it would be a great three-part series that the station would heavily promote on-air and in-print as: *Tony's Travels and Baltimore's goodwill ambassador go to Switzerland.* Not doubting that Art was moved by the potential goodwill and spirit of the mission, I knew he also realized that the compelling stories would air in the upcoming May Ratings Book. The success in that sweeps period determines the advertising rate the station can charge for the rest of the year. But, whatever the motive behind it, I was on my way to Switzerland.

My friend and photographer Jack Miller and I boarded a plane from BWI airport to Zurich. During our stay, we captured some very inspirational moments, as the little bald-headed boy from Baltimore made the rounds on the floor of the Zurich children's hospital. Even though many of the children spoke no English, there were smiles, handshakes and hugs, expressing a common bond of support and love for each other. There was also time for fun on our trip. After taking a train ride up the snow-covered Alps, Chris and I frolicked through the powdery white stuff. And, of course, when in Switzerland do like the Swiss do, so the two of us belted out our best yodeling. *Yodel- a he hoo.* We laughed as we heard our joyful echoes.

The results from our international reports were everything we had hoped for and more. It chronicled the inspirational life of a little boy who wouldn't allow his fight with cancer to defuse his courageous spirit. The three-part series not only generated an outpouring of favorable comments from viewers, but the Associated Press also awarded it the honor of being the top TV feature story of the year in Maryland.

The week away in Switzerland was the longest period of time that Sandy and I had been apart. When I returned, we had heart-to-heart talks about where our relationship was headed. As much as I had all along talked about never wanting to get married again, our mutual feelings for each other soon seemed destined to change all that.

11

SINGING MY HEART OUT FOR BRIAN AND MY CF FRIENDS

Our top notch station promotions lady, Maria Velleggia, stopped by my desk and asked, "How would you like to sing on stage at the State Fair, in front of a big audience?"

Now, in my TV stories, I had been known to burst into song on certain occasions, as I did with Mayor Schaefer more than once. But the Maryland State Fair featured big-name performers each year, so where would I fit in? Maria explained that the local country radio station was hosting a media singing contest that would take place on the big stage prior to the headline act. *Sounds tempting,* I thought, *but I hardly know any country songs and I would hate to embarrass myself by trying to croon a tune in front of all those folks.* Maria interrupted, "Did I tell you the winner of the contest gets a brand-new sports car, which he must agree to donate to his favorite charity?"

"Hmmm, it looks like I need to get some boots and a cowboy hat." After becoming good buddies with Brian Gray, he introduced me to a number of other children with cystic fibrosis. Every time I would do a story about them or the work being done by the Maryland CF chapter, it would break my heart to think about the fate the children faced. That's why I agreed to be a CF board member and do whatever I could to help raise both awareness and money for the cause. If somehow I could win the singing contest, I'd sign over the car to the CF foundation. It would, in turn, be able to sell the new car for about $15,000.

Brian, my CF friends and their families were thrilled at the prospect, but, first thing's first, I needed to come up with a song. With a month to go before the contest, I began listening to country radio a lot. I knew I didn't have the smooth sound of an Alan Jackson or the soothing style of George Strait. But, one day, driving along in my car, the DJ says, "Here's Hank Jr. with *All my Rowdy Friends*." After hearing the first thirty seconds of the rocking country party tune, I knew I had found my song. I had a chance to rehearse with the local country band that would be providing the backup music for all eight celebrity contestants. I felt my stiffest competition would be from the very popular TV 13 Weather personality Marty Bass, who was singing a parody entitled all *My Ex's Live in Essex*.

The night of the show the grandstand at the fair was packed with howling fans. As I waited my turn backstage, I tried to calm the butterflies that were flying deep down in my gut. You might wonder why someone who had been on TV so long would be so nervous. Keep in mind that, in TV, we seldom see our audience face-to-face or get immediate feedback from them. Then… *LADIES AND GENTLEMEN FROM, WMAR CHANNEL TWO — HERE'S TONY PAGNOTTI!*

The butterflies instantly flew away at the sound of hands clapping and feet stomping. Feeding off the crowd's energy, I felt like I was Bocephus himself, on stage, belting out the lyrics in tempo with the band's pulsating rhythm.

DO YOU WANNA DANCE?

DO YOU WANT TO PARTY?

HEY THIS IS ROCKING, RAMBLIN' PAG, READY TO GET THE FAIR STARTED. I GOT A PIG IN THE GROUND, BEER ON ICE AND ALL MY ROWDY FRIENDS ARE AT THE STATE FAIR TONIGHT.

And talk about a finishing with a big splash on the last note. I jumped from the stage and into the first row of the audience. Sure enough, I won the contest and the car.

The next day, I picked Brian up in the spiffy sports car and taped a *Tony's Travels* for that night's news. The CF foundation would sell the car for fifteen grand, and that money would then be used to find a cure for the number one genetic killer of children in our country. I was thrilled thinking how that would help in ending the disease someday. But I was saddened, too, in realizing that a cure would not come in time to save Brian and other CF kids his age.

The author, age 22, on set at WLOS-TV Asheville, N.C.in 1976, on his maiden voyage of becoming a Broadcast Journalist. (Tony Pagnotti personal files)

Tony reporting live for WNBC-TV in Midtown Manhattan at a unior labor protest. (Tony Pagnotti personal files)

The two Italian Stallions meet at 30 Rock, NYC in 1983. Ok smile and say provolone. (Tony Pagnotti personal files)

Hanging at Hurley's Tavern (Studio 1 H) with iconic WNBC anchor woman Sue Simmons and New York's first African American TV journalist Bob Teague. I learned to cope with the common place job insecurity of TV from Bob who cautioned his colleagues : "We Love you..We Love you..We Love you..YOU'RE FIRED!"

The author as long time host of the WMAR-TV MDA Labor Day Telethon celebrating in 1996 with news anchor Keith Cate, Telethon Ambassador Sarah Collier and news anchor Sherry Jones. (photo courtesy of Stuart Zolotorow)

Tony lending legendary comedian and iconic Telethon host Jerry Lewis a shoulder to laugh on during an unscripted rehearsal moment (photo courtesy of Stuart Zolotorow)

I learned so much about Cystic Fibrosis and living life to the fullest from my friend Brian Gray. Here in 1986 along side his Mom Pat, I was humbled when he presented me with CF Foundation of Maryland Media Recognition Award.

The author and Orioles legend Brooks Robinson at Dream Week in Clearwater Fla. 1987 where Tony learned from the Hall of Famer on how to get to 3rd base. At camp, our intrepid reporter was chastised by Earl Weaver after inviting the irascible manager to sing a chorus of "Orioles Magic".

Tony at the Walters Art Gallery Volunteers Awards Ceremony in 1998 introducing Governor William Donanld Schaefer... who introduced Tony to wife Sandy.

FOX 5 NEWS **TONY PAGNOTTI**
METEOROLOGIST

Author promotional headshot in 2018 as weekend weathercaster on FOX 45
Baltimore. (Photo courtesy of Sinclair Broadcast Group)

12

ANOTHER CONTEST FOR A GOOD CAUSE- AND GUESS WHO'S THE TOP PRIZE?

Does the anchorman delivering the news to you have any pants on? How's that for another attention-grabbing tease? The truth of the matter is that you see most anchor people from the waist up when they're sitting on the news set. So, I'll let you in on a dirty little secret of TV news: many anchormen that you see, dressed in expensive Italian suits with vests and silk ties, are possibly wearing either shorts or jeans. The thought process behind the half-dressed look is that, since you can't see below the desk, why wear uncomfortable formal pants during all those hours spent in the newsroom prior to airtime?

Even though a weatherman has to be standing up in front of the Chroma key map, he can still get away with wearing shorts or jeans and sneakers by asking the cameraman to frame his entire presentation from the waist up. But TV talent has to be careful not to take too many liberties with on-air appearances, as an anchor's public image can make or break a career. That's why all anchorman on TV wear makeup on-air. While in New York, we had makeup artists to do the job. In most other markets, it's up to the anchors to buy their own basic pancake and powder foundation and apply it themselves, just before airtime. After finishing many weekend shows, I would rush back to my apartment, where I'd meet Sandy.

One night, we were sitting on the sofa sipping wine and listening to music. The ambiance was just right. But after coming back from the bathroom, Sandy sat at the far end of the sofa. When I asked her if everything was ok, she said, "Yes," but I knew something was wrong. After a few awkward, silent moments, she told me she was upset because, on my bathroom sink, she saw a bottle of some other woman's makeup. When I told her it belonged to me and that makeup supplies for men are tools of the TV trade, we had a good laugh.

Anyone dating a person who works in TV has to be open minded about the individual's role and relationship with the public. Part of my commitment is to use the clout of being a recognizable local celebrity to help out charitable causes. But when the *American Lung Association* invited me to be a part of a fundraiser, "Bid for Bachelors," I was reluctant. The fundraising concept was to have Baltimore's ten most high-profile eligible bachelors auctioned off to the highest bidders at an auction party at the Hyatt Inner

Harbor. Even though it sounded like a lot of fun for a great cause, I didn't really consider myself an eligible bachelor since I was in a serious relationship. After talking it over with Sandy, we both agreed that the ladies bidding would be looking to support the *Lung Association* and were not in search of love and romance.

So, there I was, on stage with my fellow bachelors, all in tuxedos, and the bidding got underway. About a hundred women took part in the lively proceedings. The women were in great spirits, thanks to three hours of open bars. The winning bids were averaging in the 100 to 500 dollar range. But when it came to my turn, I was both delighted and a bit embarrassed, particularly with Sandy looking on, that the bidding was going strong at $1,000. What I did notice was that, each time the auctioneer was about to say, "Going once, twice," the same woman kept driving the price higher.

"Tony Pagnotti, sold to the woman in the pink dress for $1,500.00."

I went up to her and thanked her for being so generous. She was pretty, well-dressed and looked to be about five years older than me. I told her the station's promotion department would be in touch with her to set up our date. As Sandy and I left the festivities, she congratulated me on getting the highest bid of the night and then asked, smiling "So, where are you going on your date?

I told Maria, our promotions director, that a catered picnic lunch date would be nice and that I'd have it taped as part of *Tony's Travels*. A few days later, Maria said that, before she would agree to our formal picnic date, my winning bidder wanted me to personally call her and set up a preliminary date to get to know each other.

"That's not going to happen," I replied. "Agreeing to participate in a public fundraiser does not carry over into my private life."

Upon hearing this, the bachelorette called the *Lung Association* and threatened to stop payment on her check, as she felt I wasn't giving her what she purchased at auction. In the end, she agreed to pay half of her bid, $750.00. Begrudgingly she agreed to picnic with me on what you could imagine was a rather awkward date. Lesson learned, from that day forward I stuck to more traditional fundraising events, such as the annual Jerry Lewis Labor Day Telethon.

13

JERRY LEWIS, YOU'VE GOT TO BE KIDDING (1988)

As a co-host of the twenty-one hour spectacular with the beautiful and bubbly Beverly Burke I got to meet more inspirational children and their families. The Channel 2 studios were turned into party central, with games, festivities, volunteers manning the phones and taking pledges and a giant tote board that would tally up hourly figures. Despite going without sleep for several hours, an adrenaline rush would keep me pumped, knowing that, through the power of TV, I was helping make an impact in other peoples' lives. Leading up to the telethon, stations from around the country sent their telethon hosts to Las Vegas to participate in the MDA workshops and promo photo sessions. Besides being briefed on the latest updates on research and other relevant data used during the telethon, we got a chance to shoot promos with the man himself, Jerry.

Despite his extreme generosity and commitment to the MDA cause over the years, Jerry has been known to have a nasty streak about him, especially when the cameras weren't rolling. The first year I attended the seminar in Vegas, I stood in line with about one hundred hosts from around the country. We were all dressed in our finest TV attire, waiting for Mr. Lewis to show up so that we each could read a scripted promo with him, for use back home by our affiliated stations. When he finally entered the room, I was taken aback by two things. First, he looked like he had just come from the pool, wearing a T-shirt and shorts, and had a look that told me he would still rather be poolside. Second, he was barking orders at the show's producers and crew on how exactly he wanted things set up before he would begin the shoot.

Once everything was to his liking, a cue card was placed by the side of a camera with a generic promo in which each host's name would be inserted. When it came my turn, Jerry saw my name on the card and said, "Oh, Paglioti, a paisano huh?"

"Yeah, I'm Italian, but it's pronounced Pag-not-ee."

He squinted and looked up again at the cards, then said, "Oh, Pag-a-lot-ee."

"Close, but not quite."

"Whatever," he barked. "Let's go. Roll tape. Hi, I'm Jerry Lewis, getting ready for the annual MDA Labor Day telethon with Baltimore's Tony Pagliotti, ah, Pagriotti, or something like that."

Then I finished out by saying, "Join us, here on WMAR TV, friends you can turn to."

"Ok, next," Lewis looked beyond me to the next host in line.

I asked, "Can we re-do that real quickly so we have a clean pronunciation of my name?"

"No, kid, that's comedy. I did that on purpose. People back in Baltimore will think that's a funny bit."

With no other option, I brought the taped promo home. Our station's general manager didn't think it was amusing. "You go all the way to Vegas to get a promo with him and he doesn't have the decency to pronounce your name right. We're not going to use that promo on air." Even before this encounter with the ornery entertainer, I was never a big fan of him as a performer. But I still have to credit him with being one of show business's top philanthropists.

14

COMING FACE-TO-FACE WITH A FIGURE FROM THE PAST WHO ALMOST RUINED MY FUTURE (1992)

A memo went out to all Channel 2 staffers that the company had hired a new consultant and that the President of *TV FOCUSED RESEARCH* would be visiting the newsroom to introduce himself. When I saw the name Bill Boyer, I thought, *this guy may not need to introduce himself to me.* Could this be the same guy from the Masters Company who suggested I should get out of TV, back when I was a rookie reporter in Asheville? Sure enough, I saw Ed escorting the infamous Boyer around the office. His hair had gotten gray over the years, but there was no mistaking that this was the man who had almost ruined my career several years earlier.

With a big, toothy grin, he extended his arm and said "Hi, I'm Bill Boyer."

"Yes, Bill, I know. Remember me? From WLOS TV, when you were a junior consultant?"

"Oh, that's right, Tony. I knew you looked familiar. Well, I started my own company a few years ago and I'm glad we'll be working together again."

"Yeah, and to think, I might not still be in the business these days if I'd listened to you." His big smile turned into a frown as I continued. "Do you remember pulling me aside and telling me how I wasn't cut out for TV, and that I should consider another occupation?"

"I… I said that?" he stuttered and gave me an incredulous look. "Well, I was young, myself, and made some mistakes along the way."

"Well, Bill, after that conversation, I went home and cried and almost packed it in the next day."

Seeing the hurt in my eyes, he said, "Sorry. I'm glad you went on to prove me wrong."

Looking back, I'm actually one of the lucky ones who've had similar consultant encounters. I know of several talented, hard-working people with whom I have worked over the years who were fired by station management acting on the recommendation of an outside consultant. Unfortunately, one of the downsides to being on TV is the subjectivity that goes into evaluating on-air talent. An anchorman or woman can be told that he or she is being let go because of Q ratings or poor performance in focus groups that were conducted. These focus groups are formed when consultants select a random group of people in a TV market and have them comment on video clips of on-air talent.

The focus groups are asked to rate the anchors on such subjective evaluations as likeability, credibility and sincerity. It's the outcome of these assessments that often determines whether an anchor's contract is renewed or if the anchor will be unceremoniously fired. Often times, when the talent is let go, that anchor does a final newscast without ever saying goodbye. That leaves a confused audience asking, "Whatever happened to—?" In the here-to-day-gone-tomorrow world of TV news, the toppled talent that was made to feel like chopped liver will either wind up in another TV market and be touted "as the greatest thing since sliced bread," or will end up resigning himself or herself to the fact that a TV career is toast and it's time for a new line of work.

For a number of on-air folk, including myself, broadcasting is all we have ever done. The thought of getting a real job someday is both appealing and appalling. Those broadcasters who have done so say how great it is to finally work a nine-to-five day, with weekends and holidays off, and not be in a business where job security is tied to Arbitron sweeps books and Q ratings. Conversely, despite the daily demands and pressures that go along with being a TV personality, there is no heavy lifting required, nor is one expected to have completed assigned tasks and projects at the end of each day. Ultimately, the talent is the product. Of the eight hours spent at the TV station each day, a fraction of the time is spent in front of the camera. But it's those precious performance moments of connecting to an audience that matters most.

There was a time in TV news when anchors were expected to go out in the field and cover a story between the 6 and 11 broadcasts. News directors not only felt that they were getting their money's worth out of their highly-paid anchors, but they also believed viewers would perceive that the anchorperson was a hard-working journalist, not just some pretty face reading the news. But the reality is that many anchors have little or no reporting background. They were hired to look and sound good while reading a teleprompter. But, frankly, reading from a script WITH CAPITAL LETTERS from only five feet away is not all that easy to master.

Unlike when reading an optometrist's eye chart, a good anchor doesn't stare straight ahead and read without blinking an eye. Viewers have seen inexperienced anchors using this deer-in-headlights style of reading, and it looks terrible. Top-notch talent flawlessly breezes through the prompter copy while occasionally looking down at the hard copy script they are holding. Anchors are supposed to keep their script pages turning at the same pace as the automated prompter script. But, every now and then, a camera lens prompter goes out during a live newscast and the anchor must keep on reading from the desk copy, provided the copy is in the right order. Viewers can instantly tell when an anchor gets caught with the teleprompter down, when, with reddened face an anchor starts frantically shuffling through the script, looking to find the story supposedly being read. As it's live TV, an anchor can't just look up and say, "Sorry, folks, I lost my place. Just bear with me for a minute until I get my bearings or they get the damned teleprompter fixed."

Some anchors become so tied to a teleprompter that they demand the producer script every single word from the "Good Evening" to the "Good Night," and all the so called "ad libs" in between. Believe it or not, I have worked with some anchors who, when leading into my weather, will look at the prompter and read, *IT HAS BEEN A CLOUDY DAY, WILL WE NEED OUR UMBRELLAS TOMORROW,* and *TONY PAGNOTTI IS HERE WITH WHAT LOOKS TO BE A WET FORECAST.* I've been tempted to respond, "No, it's not going to rain, and where did you get that erroneous information? Listen up for the next three minutes and I'll give you the forecast."

By the way, I've never actually worked with an anchor who listened while I was doing the weather. Anchors look at the weather segment as a time to drink some water, look in a compact mirror to check makeup, or, in a hushed voice, pick up the studio desk phone and order Chinese takeout for after the show. It never fails. After finishing a newscast, my anchor colleague will look at me with a straight-face and ask, "So, is it going to rain tomorrow?"

In reality, all that most viewers want is a quick forecast to let them know how to dress themselves or the kids. That info can be provided in thirty seconds. But all research shows that the majority of people tune in to their local news for the weather. You'll notice that weather segments are strategically placed right after the top news stories of the day. After feeding you the daily dosage of gloom-and-doom, your TV friends want to lift you from the depths of depression by presenting the always bright-and-cheery weathercaster who reassures you, "Grey skies are going to clear up, so put on a happy face." And let it be known that, unlike news and sports anchors, the weather segment isn't scripted. Think of it as a sophisticated show and tell, as we ad lib our way around satellite/radar images, meteorological computer models and various forecasting graphics.

This brings me back to my earlier point of the teleprompter being the news anchor's trusted friend. Whatever is written on the prompter's script will be communicated to the viewing audience. In some instances, an anchor will not take the time to pre-read the script before going live. At the beginning of one particular 6 PM news on Channel 2, the opening theme music played, and co-anchors Rick Douglas and Maureen Noone waited for their opening cue. As soon as the floor director pointed in their direction, Maureen read, *"GOOD EVENING EVERYONE, I'M RICK DOUGLAS. OUR TOP STORY TONIGHT.* Rick's jaw dropped, not believing that his co-anchor just introduced herself as him. After the newscast, the newsroom was flooded with calls from viewers wondering if Maureen even knew her own name. There is a common mantra that we TV talent live by: 'YOU'RE ONLY AS GOOD AS YOUR LAST BROADCAST.' Maureen Noone (aka Rick Douglas) didn't last long after that blooper was heard 'round Baltimore.

15

PROPOSING A PRECIPITOUS QUESTION

After two years in Baltimore, life was good both on and off TV. Besides enjoying my celebrity status in Charm City, I felt I had found a wonderful woman who would cause me to break my promise to myself and get married again. I decided a romantic time to pop the question would be on Christmas Eve. But as I looked at the calendar, I realized there was a conflict. I was scheduled to do weather that night at both 6 and 11. After not being able to get my weather colleague to fill in for me, I still decided to go ahead with my plan and invited Sandy to meet me at my apartment during my dinner break. As soon as the camera's red light went off, ending the 6 PM show, I rushed home. I got the diamond ring out of my underwear drawer where I had been hiding it for the past several weeks and put it in my shirt pocket. When Sandy arrived, we made a Christmas Eve toast and had dinner. I was feeling nervous, wondering what I should say if, by chance, she said "No." No sooner did we finish eating than I said, "I have a Christmas present I'd like to give you now."

She opened the small gift box and saw the shiny diamond. With tears in her eyes, she screamed, "Oh, my God!"

"So, you *will* marry me?"

We kissed and hugged, and I apologized that our engagement celebration would have to be put on hold until 11:30. Newly engaged or not, this dedicated broadcaster would have to temporarily leave his bride-to-be. After all, viewers were awaiting my word on whether or not they could expect a white Christmas in Baltimore.

Just as with a successful author, artist, or singer, a TV performer must develop a distinct style that is embraced by the public. The best anchors and reporters that I have worked with over the years are those who have pretty much the same personality both on and off the air. Sure, there are those who, in their private lives, are unlikable individuals, but who are able to turn on an appealing persona once the camera light goes on. But it has been my experience that this type of talent can fake it on air for only so long before an audience sees through the facade. There is a difference between phoniness and performance. When viewers watch TV news, they should keep in mind that the on-air folks are in a studio with lights, reading from a script and wearing makeup. Sounds like show business to me. That's why an anchorperson has to be more than "just his- or herself on air." In order to project the proper on-air energy and enthusiasm, we TV personalities, must pump up our off-air persona with the right amount of facial animation, vocal inflection and compelling non-verbal communication.

Seeing a favorite TV personality in a grocery store, one can see that the charisma visual on the tube each night is missing. That's because in everyday life, the TV person doesn't feel the need to be "on" during a day off from work. But persons in such high-profile jobs must be prepared for public scrutiny. There have been times over the years when I have been out and about, trying to be Tony Q Public, and I heard the following comments from my adoring audience: "You look better, fatter, taller, older, and younger on TV than you do in person." Not knowing what the appropriate response was, I usually smiled and said thanks for watching. Then, there was the time I was pumping gas and, like anyone else, just staring blankly at the rapidly moving numbers on the pump. I looked up and a woman at the adjoining pump staring at me shouted, "Gee, Tony, you look so serious. Why aren't you smiling like you always do on TV?" Conditioned like Pavlov's dog, I produced a big smile and waved but wondered if she would go and tell her friends, "You know, I saw that Tony Pagnotti at the gas station and he didn't look like the happy-go-lucky guy I see on TV."

But I've been able to grin and bear all the public attention that goes with the TV territory, especially since being a local celebrity pays off. Recently, I was speeding home after dropping my daughter off at James Madison University in Virginia. About a half hour from my house, I saw flashing lights in my rearview mirror. The officer walked up to my window and told me he clocked me going seventy-two miles per hour in a fifty mile per hour zone. I handed him my driver's license and his frown was replaced by smile. "Hey, Mr. Tony, I've been watching you for years on TV."

Instead of handing me a ticket he gave me a handshake and a reminder to drive carefully.

During the first few years at Channel 2, what made my job so great was that management let me do and say whatever I wished in my roles as weatherman and *Tony's Travels* reporter. The positive, high-profile approach I used in both capacities resulted in me being the station's goodwill ambassador. I found myself as the emcee at various events along the banquet trail. I tried to accommodate as many requests as possible without spreading myself to thin. Most requests came by mail, but, then, there was the day when I received a very special phone call.

The caller, with a deep voice and southern drawl, began: "Hello, young man. I've been watching you on TV for a couple years now and appreciate all the good you're doing in our neighborhoods. You're a man after my own heart, and I need for you to come to my little breakfast and introduce the fine folks next month. Can this old country boy count on you, partner?"

"Sure," I replied.

"Much obliged, my brother." He hung up.

After making the on-the-spot commitment, I figured I should find something out about what I was getting myself into. After a few phone calls, I discovered the little breakfast was a huge event. The *Fullwood Foundation* Caring and Sharing breakfast attracted over 1,000 guests. Harlow Fullwood was a Baltimore philanthropist who made his money back in the 1960s when he became one of Kentucky Fried Chicken's first minority franchise owners in the country. At the breakfast, he awarded thousands of dollars in college scholarships to needy high schoolers. The breakfast, also honoring individuals who were making differences in the community, had the feel-good atmosphere and brotherhood of a gospel revival. I felt blessed to be a part of it all. That day also marked the start of what would be a longtime friendship with the big-hearted, old country boy from North Carolina.

Some of the best *Tony's Travels* and subsequent friendships began with viewer phone calls. I often heard from proud parents who would ask me to feature their talented children on *Tony's Travels*. I would usually thank them politely for calling and would keep their contact info on file. But, every now and then, if I sensed something special about their parental pitch, I agreed to do a feature story that just might launch their kids to a career of stardom.

One time, the man on the other end of the line said he was a minister and the proud papa of five singing sisters, ranging from eleven to eighteen. He told me they began singing in his church in grade school and now had a cassette of their singing that they hoped some record producer might be interested in. Photographer Jack Miller and I met the girls in the family basement where they were harmonizing around the piano. They had a beautiful, spiritual, contemporary sound and came across as poised and professional during my on-camera interview. As was the case with my features, I ended the segment by presenting them with *Tony's Travels* T-shirts. They responded in perfect harmony: "Thank you, Tony." Upon leaving, I wished them well and asked them to keep me posted about their pursuit of stardom.

139

About a year later, one of the station photographers stopped me in the hall and asked, "Do remember the singing sisters you did a story on?"

"Sure, I do. What are they doing these days?"

"Well," he said, "I don't know what four of them are up to, but their oldest sister has a smash hit song, and it's being played on the radio all over the country."

Gee, I thought, *I guess Toni Braxton must have forgotten to share her good news with the TV reporter who not only gave her first exposure on TV, but also gave her a coveted* Tony's Travels *T-shirt.* The sultry-voiced Severn, Maryland girl went on to become a Grammy-winning international recording star. To this day, I often wonder if she still has her *Tony's Travels* T-shirt. And if she does, I imagine her chauffer is using it to wipe down her limousine.

16

MATRIMONY: TAKE TWO

October 10, 1987. Sandy and I exchanged "I dos" at Trinity Lutheran Church in Reisterstown, Maryland. Following the service, we hosted a wedding celebration for about two hundred of our family members, friends, and colleagues at Martin's Banquet Hall in Westminster. It was great to have all those people who meant so much to me there.

Sandy and I were moved that Brian Gray was able to make it. The cystic fibrosis had caused his condition to deteriorate. But he told me he wouldn't miss being at our wedding for anything, especially since I had asked him to introduce us when it came time to sing our special song. Yes, since we had a live band and a captive audience I couldn't resist doing a rendition of the song that won me the car at the state fair. So, accompanied by my wife, the crowd went crazy when we belted out:

> *Got to be happy, it feels so right cause all our rowdy friends are at our wedding tonight.*

Our guests demanded an encore and the vivacious Sally Thorner led the chant "one more time." We danced and partied the night away. The festivities were videotaped by a photographer we hired for the occasion. More than a few friends asked when I would be showing wedding highlights on Channel 2. Even though I knew viewers would get a kick out of seeing the marriage merriment, I decided to keep this private slice of my life just that – private.

After settling into married life, one of the first things Sandy and I decided to do was to sell my condo and buy a new home. For that to happen, we needed to go over our budget and see where to tighten the belt on expenses. The first thing to jump out at us was that I was under contract to pay six percent of my yearly salary to Carole Cooper and would continue to do so as long as I was working in TV. While I was grateful for her finding me the Baltimore job, I felt I would be content staying at Channel 2 for years to come and didn't anticipate the need for an agent's services. So, I called Carole and explained that, as much as I hated to part ways with her agency, I had to in order to make a down payment on a new house. She explained that, legally, she could hold me to our contractual agreement, but, reluctantly, she would agree to my request. As I thanked her for all she had done for me, she warned me that, even though things might be rosy for now, the TV biz is fickle. "Best of luck to you Tony, but if, down the road you find you find yourself searching for another job, please don't call me, because I won't be able to take you back." As I hung up the phone, I wondered if what I had just done was equivalent to cancelling a life insurance policy.

17

AN IRATE ANCHOR EXERCISES HIS CONSTITUTIONAL RIGHTS

Speaking of contracts, my three-year deal with Channel 2 was nearing its end. Since I was no longer represented by Carole Cooper, I asked a good friend to handle the negotiations. Tony Agnone is a Baltimore-based agent who represents a number of NFL players including Michael Strahan and some local TV news people. I met Tony shortly after moving to Baltimore. We became fast friends, and he was a groomsman at my wedding. Tony agreed to meet with my GM to work out a new three-year contract. Tony confided that, since I now had one of the highest Q ratings in the market, he could go into the meeting with strong bargaining power. Sure enough, after less than an hour, Tony had gotten me a new three-year contract agreement that included a thirty percent pay increase. With that, all systems were go to build a new home in Owings Mills.

It was just a few weeks after signing my new contract that I attended a party at my super agent's house. There, I met some of the TV folks from the other stations in town. People seem to think that, just because someone's on local television, he knows the other broadcasters in town. Unless we happen to run into each other out doing the same story, we, like the viewers, only know each other from being seen on television. Standing near the bar was a tall, thin man with brown hair and a dark complexion who I immediately recognized as a reporter from another local station. In his late forties, Will was a longtime reporter in the market. After I introduced myself, the veteran broadcaster and I started talking about the crazy world of TV News.

Will said he wound up in Baltimore after he got screwed by management at a station he had been working at as a prime time anchor.

Before I could ask what happened, the reminiscing reporter was taking me back to the scene of the crime, ten years earlier. "You see, I had been anchoring at the ABC affiliate in Birmingham, Alabama, for about two and a half years when I read in my contract that the station had an out clause it could use to not renew me. Now, at just about that time, my wife and I were getting ready to build a new house in town. But before we moved forward, I went to the General Manager and asked if my contract would be renewed. He assured me there was nothing to worry about. Well, four months later we got the mail." As he continued his face turned bright red and his voice filled with anger.

"The letter was from the GM who wrote 'that due to unexpected economic conditions, the station would not be able to renew my contract.' I couldn't believe what I was reading. By the end of the month, I would be out of a job and faced with the prospect of the bank foreclosing on our house. If I had owned a gun, I would have been tempted to shoot that bastard.

"I was filled with rage and wanted revenge. That night, I went into the station and headed to the prick's third-floor office. It looked like he had left for the day, but his door was open. With no one else in sight, I walked into his plush office and stood behind his mahogany desk. I proceeded to drop my drawers to my knees, assumed a squatting position, and took a big, smelly dump on his desk." He punctuated his story with a hearty laugh and added, "Since he thought it was okay to shit on me, I decided to return the favor."

"I kid you not," he concluded. "I walked out of that station, never to be seen again."

To this day I wonder if the station ever considered filing a lawsuit against him, perhaps for defecation of character.

18

ANOTHER BOSS (AND FORMER BUNK MATE) GOES PACKING

It's probably apparent to the reader that the TV business is very transient. But it's not just the anchors and reporters that tend to hopscotch from city to city. News directors are also in the line of fire when it comes to getting laid off. The boss of the newsroom is usually sent packing for one of two reasons: either the ratings are down or stagnant, or there is a falling-out between him and the general manager. I'm not sure if either of those resulted in Ed's dismissal.

All of us were shocked when he put out a two-line memo, stating that he had enjoyed the five years he spent as news director, but he would be leaving the station to pursue other interests. He remained tightlipped about his decision to leave and if it was, in fact, his decision. On his last day, I wished him well and pledged to keep our intoxicating interview extravaganza a secret until the day when I wrote my book. His unexpected exit had me suddenly contemplating how the move might impact my future. It's always been my belief that in the topsy-turvy world of TV, when the guy who hired you leaves, there are no guarantees that the new boss will feel the same about you as the old boss.

Within a few weeks, it was rumored that our interim news director would be Gary Wordlaw, who had previously been the station's operations manager. In that position, Gary was in charge of purchasing station equipment and supplies, along with overseeing the fleet of company news vehicles. Before coming to Baltimore, his news experience had been as a producer-reporter at TV stations. Gary was a very likeable guy, knew the Baltimore market and was always coming up with innovative and promotable ideas. He was the one responsible for buying the hundreds of *Tony's Travels* T-shirts, complete with a caricature of yours truly riding in a sports car that I not-so-humbly gave out during my travels.

Just about the time that many of us started wondering if Gary might be named the permanent news director, it was announced that an outsider had been given the job. John Shamsky had a reputation for being a proven newsroom leader and good guy. He certainly lived up to his billing immediately. In an effort to get to know the news staff, he made it a point to talk to each of us individually.

He certainly made points with me when he said he had watched tapes of our newscasts and was a big fan of my weather forecasts and *Tony's Travels* features.

We both shared the same philosophy: that TV news was at its best whenever the intimacy of the medium was used to make a difference in people's everyday lives. Within six months John won over the newsroom with the passion and commitment he brought to the job.

Weighing around 350 pounds, John was a bear of a man. Less than a year after being our likeable leader, suddenly Shamsky's office light was off more than it was on.

In the weeks that followed, he called in sick frequently. The word was he had been trying a few different diets and they were making him ill. Then, on one such sick day, a memo came out, reading, "Effective immediately, John Shamsky is resigning his position as news director. We wish him well in his future endeavors." The buzz around the station was that his health was failing. . I was sad to see him go and couldn't help but wonder who would be named our next news director. "Meet the New Boss, Same as the Old Boss," as the refrain goes, from rock band The Who. Gary Wordlaw was now in charge.

19

FAREWELL TO A DEAR YOUNG FRIEND AND WELCOMING A BABY GIRL

March 18, 1988 is one date that I will never forget, because it marked one of my saddest days ever. That's the day I got the call that I hoped would never come but always knew was inevitable. Brian Gray died. His mother fought back tears while telling me that my fourteen-year-old friend went peacefully as she held him in her arms. Then, I had to go into the station and carry out one of my toughest assignments in my career. I sat in a dark editing room and looked over past stories of Brian that would be part of a memorial tribute story I would introduce live on set. I actually found the screening process helpful in easing my grief. I sat there, smiling, as I watched the fun we had in Disneyworld, him throwing out the first pitch at the Orioles home opener, the two of us walking together as part of a relay fundraiser for CF and me driving Brian around in the car I had won at the fair for the Cystic Fibrosis foundation. It made me realize how, despite the bad hand he had been dealt in life, Brian never complained. He lived life to the fullest. When it came time for me to introduce the taped tribute, I walked into the studio, put on my microphone, took a deep breath, looked into the camera and delivered a heartfelt sendoff which I'm sure had my buddy looking down on me and smiling in approval.

My feeling is that, just like in pro sports, if you have a solid team with good players and a solid coaching staff, the manager has little impact on overall performance. Since our news programs were doing very well in the ratings, I hoped that our newly-named news director wouldn't do anything to mess things up. Gary adhered to the old philosophy, "If it ain't broke, don't try and fix it." One day, he called me in his office and said, "How would you like for *Tony's Travels* to be live from Disneyworld in a few months for the grand opening of MGM studios, the newest part of the park?"

When I told Sandy that night of my exciting news, she wasn't exactly jumping up and down. That wouldn't be a good thing for a woman who was seven months pregnant to do. We were expecting our first child around May 10. The Disney trip was scheduled for the prior week. Being a first-time father, I assumed there would be no conflict. I would be back with five days to spare.

"But what if the baby arrives early and you're down in Disneyworld?" Sandy was, naturally, worried.

Not wanting to miss the birth of the baby for anything in the world, I went into Wordlaw's office and told him I wouldn't be able to make the trip for the risk of missing my child's arrival in the world.

Gary shot back, "No, you will be going. Don't worry. Tell your wife your producer be wearing a pager at all times. If, by chance, there are indications she is going to deliver early, have her call me and I'll have you on the next plane back to Baltimore."

So, when the time came, I was off to Florida, praying that the stork's delivery would not be early. Fortunately, my prayers were answered. I returned back home on May 5. Three days later with my home camcorder in hand, I was there in the delivery room when Alessandra Ann Pagnotti was born. It is an intensive emotional experience to witness the miracle of your child's birth.

The Channel 2 audience got a chance that night to see our brand new bundle of joy. It is standard procedure for most stations that, when an anchorman or woman has a baby, a station videographer is sent to the proud parent's hospital room in order to take the pictures which will be shown as the kicker for the newscast.

Sally intro: AND FINALLY TONIGHT, WE ARE HAPPY TO WELCOME THE NEWEST MEMBER OF THE CHANNEL TWO NEWS FAMILY...

TONY PAGNOTTI AND HIS WIFE, SANDY, ARE THE PROUD PARENTS OF A BABY GIRL. HERE IS THE BEAUTIFUL ALESSANDRA ANN PAGNOTTI WHO WAS BORN THIS AFTERNOON AT GBMC, WEIGHING EIGHT POUNDS AND SEVEN OUNCES. TONY HAS TRAVELLED

TO A LOT OF EXCITING PLACES, BUT HIS EXPERIENCE TODAY IN THE DELIVERY ROOM HAS TO BE HIS MOST THRILLING TRAVEL EVER. CONGRATULATIONS TO TONY AND SANDY. AND, WITH THAT, WE SAY THANK YOU AND GOOD NIGHT.

In the remaining ten seconds ending the newscast, the Channel 2 news theme music played over a final still video of my baby girl. That would be the first of several TV appearances Alee would be making in the months and years ahead. Whenever I could, I'd get her on Channel 2 with her doting dad.

The wheeling-dealing Wordlaw kept Tony traveling. It was the summer of 1990 when he stopped me in the hall and said, "Hey, Pagman, next month I'm sending you and Sandy to Alaska."

"Ok, what's the story angle?" I asked.

"Oh, you won't be doing any stories. I just want to you go and have a good time."

"All right, give me the scoop."

"Well, you see, our sales department is working with a national travel agency to run its commercials for a viewer trip to Alaska on our air. But as part of the deal, the agency wants the station to provide a personality who will go, along with his wife, to host the excursion. All you have to do is be your charming self to the adoring fans who signed up for the weeklong trip."

For Sandy and me, it would be a paid vacation. So, off we went on our Alaskan adventure, traveling with a group of a hundred viewers, primarily senior citizens. We were only two days into the trip when there was an unexpected and very sad message waiting for me at our inn, located in a small town near Fairbanks. My pal, Chris Polk, had lost his battle to cancer. I felt terrible knowing that I wouldn't be able to console Della and Mike, Chris's mom and dad, at their son's funeral. When I called back to Channel 2, I was told that, until he was informed that I was on the other side of the country, Mike had hoped I would deliver Chris's eulogy. Since I couldn't be there in person, I thought that I could perhaps record a eulogy on tape and get it back to Baltimore in time for the funeral service. So, I went into a drugstore in Fairbanks and bought the only audio cassette recorder on the shelf.

I went back to my hotel room and wrote about the courageous and inspirational ten-year-old. In place of a soundproof recording booth, I headed into the bathroom and read my tribute into my cassette recorder. With the church service less than thirty-six hours away, I was faced with the dilemma of how to get the eulogy there in time. Outside the drugstore where I bought the recorder there was dusty Federal Express drop off box that looked like it hadn't been used a lot by the locals. But I had no choice.

As I dropped the package in the box, Sandy said, "Okay, Chris, please make sure you help get this tape to the church on time."

Believe it or not it got, it to the church just in the nick of time. Even though I was upset I couldn't be there, I felt much better knowing I was able to honor Chris's memory. Mike told me that he had played the eulogy through the church speakers. From that day forward, I had newfound respect for the Fed Ex slogan, *When it absolutely positively has to be there the next day.*

But that would mark an end to my trips, since Gary announced he would be starting a new career adventure. He was hired to be news director at WJLA-TV in Washington, DC. To his credit, Worldlaw was a quick study and soon rose through management ranks in the years to come, landing prestigious VP & General Manager jobs in DC, New Orleans and Tallahassee.

Within a few weeks, I had yet another new boss. Jerry Docherty, I called a former colleague of mine who had worked with Docherty in order to find out what I could expect. "He's a no-nonsense company man who is into hard news and is not a big fan of warm and fuzzy or light-hearted feature stories." As I hung up the phone, I thought, *Gee, sorry I asked.*

Jerry certainly lived up to his billing. He would send me memos stating that he wanted my *Tony's Travels* stories that usually ran three minutes to now run no longer than two minutes. To add insult to injury, he would call me into his office after a weathercast and say he would like to see less shtick and more science in my forecasts. When I went upstairs to complain to the GM that Jack was messing with my style, he said that when Docherty was hired, he had agreed to let him run the newsroom and wouldn't challenge his decisions. Keep in mind, the end of my three-year contract was coming up in a few months.

In TV, timing is everything, in more ways than one. When I confided with our veteran anchorman, Ken Matz, that I was wondering what the future held for me, considering my less than ringing endorsements from our news director, Matz assured me I was one of the best liked personalities in Baltimore and I shouldn't worry. Famous last words.

20

WE LOVE YOU, WE LOVE YOU, WE LOVE YOU, YOU'RE FIRED! (OR SO THEY TRIED)

I was home playing with Alee when Sandy told me Tony Agnone was on the phone and didn't sound like his usual happy-go-lucky self.

"Hey, what's up, Tone?"

After a brief pause, he responded, "They're cutting you loose?"

"What do you mean?"

"Jerry called to tell me today that he isn't going to renew your contract. I was speechless and suddenly had a sick feeling in my stomach."

"But did you talk to Art Simon?

"Yeah, and he said the same bullshit about respecting his news director's decision."

I held back tears as I told Sandy the news. I looked at my playful daughter and wondered if she would be growing up in another city. After tossing and turning all night, I headed into work and marched up to office. Walking right past his secretary, I entered Art's office and sat down. With a smile, he said, "I guess Tony called you last night."

"Yes, he did, and I can't believe what he told me. This Out-of-Towner has no idea of my contributions to the station and community. But, Art, as one of my biggest supporters, you sure do. You're the GM and you can overrule the news director if you wanted to." Right then, I realized there was a chance he might also be on his way out.

"Look, I'm not going to bullshit you .Jerry told me we pay you too much and he can hire three hard news reporters on your current salary."

"But he doesn't have the decency to at least to talk to me face-to-face? He is outright firing me without even seeing if I would consider a pay cut to stay. That really pisses me off."

"Gee, Tony, you are angry. You're acting like we're sticking a sword up your ass."

"No. It's worse than that. You're sticking a sword in my heart."

With a stunned look, he said, "Look, let me talk to him and I'll get back to you tomorrow."

I immediately called Agnone and told him about my conversation. When I told him of my "knife in the heart" remark, Tony laughed and said, "It's your passion for your job that prevented him from pulling the trigger. Wait 'till he tells Docherty that your execution hasn't taken place yet."

The next day, I was back in Simon's office to get the verdict. "Ok, I went to bat for you and told him he hasn't been in Baltimore long enough to appreciate your popularity in this town. So, he has agreed to resign you to a two-year contract but with a fifty percent pay cut. I told him you probably wouldn't agree to that, but I would put it out there to you."

"Even though that is insulting, I have poured too much of myself into this job and community to be able to walk away. So, I will sign the two-year contract."

Even though I was hurt, angry and baffled over what had transpired, I had gotten myself unfired. I had to swallow my pride and consent to a fifty percent pay cut, but, as my father always told me, half a loaf is better than none. But the reality of it was that Sandy would have to go back to working full-time as a corporate events planner in order for us to keep making our monthly mortgage payments.

I didn't allow my salary slashing to have any effect on my attitude or day-to-day work. Other than an occasional 'hello' when we passed each other, Docherty and I seldom spoke. About a month later, another big management change came about that helped me better understand what went down in that office. A memo from the president of *our parent company* stated that Art Simon would be stepping down as TV 2's General Manager and would be taking a similar position at a station on the West coast. Never did I imagine I would outlast the longtime General Manager of Channel 2.

The word was that the new GM, Jim Barnes, was a longtime budget-conscious bean-counter for the company.

He had earned a reputation for going into company-owned stations with the sole intent of making them financially lean operations. Barnes himself was very a lean, tall, bespectacled man with gray hair. He wore a constant look that could be perceived as being perpetually ponderous or constantly confused. In his first meeting with station employees, he certainly lived up to his billing as being a frugal bean-counter. While he announced there would be no major changes in the news department, he said that there were two big programming alterations that had to be made. Channel 2 would no longer be the official Orioles broadcast station, and we would be dropping the Oprah Winfrey Show, the number one rated talk program in all of TV and a fantastic lead-in to our 5 and 6 PM news.

Heads turned and at least one gasp was heard following Barnes' announcement. First off, Baltimore is an Orioles-crazy town, and for thirty years people had tuned into TV 2 to see all *"dem O's"* games. Secondly, Charm City looked at the successfully syndicated Oprah as an adopted daughter, since her springboard to stardom came after making a name for herself at TV 13 in Baltimore. Sensing the staff's befuddled reaction, Barnes explained that the annual fees the station had to pay to keep the Orioles and Oprah were costing the station way too much. Within weeks, our competitor TV 11 picked up Oprah's show and Channel 13 became the Orioles station. It didn't take long for viewers to weigh in on the bonehead decisions. All of our Channel 2 news ratings went way down, while Channels 11 and 13 saw their audience numbers skyrocket.

Besides losses in ratings and revenue for the station, there was other fallout from unpopular programming moves. Viewers take their TV-watching seriously, so you have to be careful not to make a change that will result in a longstanding negative perception of the station. It is my opinion that, to this very day, it is because of that double-barrel mess up in 1991 that Channel 2 perpetually remains in the ratings cellar, having never been able to fully recover from that stupid, short-sighted decision.

21

THE HEARTBREAK OF LOSING MY # 1 FAN

The first half of 1991 was terrible for me on both a professional and personal level. My dear mother was spending a lot of time in the hospital due to diabetes complications. On my days off, I would make the three-hour trip up to Scranton and spend time with her. Despite her failing health, she always wanted to know how Sandra and that little angel Alee were doing. That was usually followed by her asking when I was going to bring her more VCR tapes of my weathercasts and *Tony's Travels*, so she could watch them in her hospital room. When I would turn the subject back to how she was feeling, her standard reply was "meza meza," Italian slang for "hanging in there."

Each visit, before I left, she would advise, "You and Sandra should enjoy that little angel Alee and not have another baby anytime soon." I knew the meaning behind that statement came from an old Italian wives' tale: *when a baby is born in a family, an elder will die in order to make room for the new arrival.* When I gave her a hug and kiss goodbye, her body seemed so frail.

On one of the drives back to Baltimore, I had an eerie feeling that I had just seen my mother alive for the last time. I didn't feel like going to work when I returned but I knew I had a *Tony's Travels* set up for that afternoon. It was a visit to a longtime family-owned candy company that specialized in making chocolate Easter bunnies and eggs. As I was getting ready to interview the merchant surrounded by his colorful creations, my mind was with my mother. As he was explaining the joy he gets from his occupation, a song playing on the radio in the background gave me chills and brought tears to my eyes. It was Stevie Wonder's, *I just called to say I love you.* Over the years, every time my mother would phone me, wherever I was living at the time, she would begin the conversation by singing those words to me. I had a feeling this time it was her dying spirit reaching out to me one last time. That night, when my phone rang at home, my premonition was confirmed.

I have been on TV thousands of times and have spoken at events before thousands of people, but my most difficult public presentation by far was delivering my mother's eulogy. The day before her funeral mass, I told my father and sister that I didn't think I could make it through a memorial speech about my mother without breaking down. But I knew my mother would want me to be the one to deliver her eulogy. Maybe it was a bit of her own divine inspiration, but reflecting on all the cherished memories our family had of her and what she meant to a legion of friends and pharmacy customers, the words all came together beautifully. At first, there was a bit of trepidation as I began my tribute before the gathering. But I reached deep down into my soul to present a celebration of life that would have made her proud.

22

TO RUSSIA WITH LOVE

As the numbers continued to get worse with each passing rating sweeps period, there was a big shakeup at the top.
Jim Barnes announced he was leaving the station to accept
a GM position at a Russian TV station.

A few days later, Jerry Docherty handed in his resignation. Now, you might think I was jumping up and down
with joy when the man who nearly fired me and then cut
my salary in half left the station. But my feeling was that the
damage he inflicted had already been done, and in time we
had come to tolerate each other. But I did feel a bit hopeful,
and thought the next guy couldn't be any worse.. Or could
he?

To add to the TV 2 woes, our longtime popular anchor
Sally Thorner made some big news herself. Apparently
when Sally's contract had come up for renewal, the station
would only agree to give her a small salary increase. When
WJZ Channel 13 heard of the impasse in Thorner's negotiations, it offered her a thirty percent increase over what
Channel 2 was offering. However, like most anchor people,

Sally had a one-year non-compete clause in her TV 2 contract which prevented her from working at TV stations in the same city where she was employed. Stations insist on such a clause in order to prevent TV talent from building up a following and then jumping to the competition. When Sally's agent told Channel 13 that, legally, Sally couldn't appear on their airwaves until the one-year non-compete clause was up, management made an astounding offer. Channel 13 said it wanted her services badly enough that they she could leave Channel 2 immediately and they would pay her a year's salary until the year was over. That meant she would be paid reportedly $250,000 for a year for just sitting home,

Nice work, if you can get it. Sally got it and remained at TV 13 for many years up until her retirement in 2008.

Several months went by, and still no new news director at Channel 2. There were days when I fantasized that if I hung in there, a new captain would come in and save the USS WMAR. But in reality I was aboard the Titanic, was headed straight toward an iceberg. Up to that point, I had already been at TV 2 twice as long as I had been at any of my previous stops, so maybe it was time to move on to a new station where my talents would be better appreciated, better utilized and better compensated. But I knew that it would have to be a pretty fantastic job opportunity to make Sandy up and move away from her family. Besides, deep down, this was the first time in my career that I felt what I was doing everyday on TV mattered. Of course, a big salary would be nice, but would I be given the same *carte blanche* by management at another station in another town?

That relocation debate almost became a moot issue when, one night at home. I received a very flattering call. The caller was Don Demerest, the news director of another station in town whom I had heard of but had never met. He got right to the point by saying that he admired my work and thought my stories were the kind viewers remember long after a newscast ended. With that, he asked if I had a non-compete clause in my contract. When I told him I did not, he continued, "Well, would you be interested in coming over to our place? You'd be prominently featured in our newscasts."

My first reaction was that one of my colleagues was pulling a prank and pretending to be the news director at Baltimore's top-rated station. But the call was authentic and I met Don for lunch later that week. We hit if off immediately, saying he had big plans for me. As our meeting ended he asked that I be patient since this was a new position he was creating just for me and it would have to be a part of his budget proposal. I was thrilled with the prospect of being able to say *arriverderci* to Channel 2 but still be on TV in Baltimore at a place that really wanted me. After a week went by, I left a voicemail for Don, saying that I was just checking in and to give me a call when he had a chance. I thought it was strange that, after another few days, I didn't get a return call. My insecurities got the best of me in my thinking that maybe his budget request for the position had been shot down. Or maybe he was busy and just didn't have the time to call and tell me he was still waiting for corporate approval.

But I discovered it was neither of those scenarios when, the next morning, I opened the Baltimore Sun entertainment section and saw this headline:

BALTIMORE NEWS DIRECTOR TAKES JOB IN ATLANTA

To my shock and dismay, Demerest was leaving to become the news director at a TV station in Georgia. Was he in the running for this position while courting me? Or did the job offer come up suddenly and he jumped at the opportunity? I tried reaching him to find out, but news room secretary said he had cleaned out his office and was gone. With that said, all hopes were dashed of me jumping ship from the TV 2 Titanic.

Christmas of 1991 was a very blessed event in the Pagnotti household. At 1:21 AM, Anna Noelle was born. As I stated earlier, when you're on TV and you have a baby, the newborn's picture, along with proud parents, are must-see TV. And, in this case, our daughter's arrival was even more newsworthy, as she was the first baby born on Christmas at the Greater Baltimore Medical Center. The nurses dressed our seven-pound-eight-ounce bambino in a Christmas stocking just in time for the Channel 2 cameraman's arrival.. Sandy said she wasn't feeling especially telegenic after just having given birth a few hours earlier but consented to the shoot in the name of good television. To make the most of special seasonal celebration, I composed for little Anna a diddy from daddy that I belted out during our photo opp.

JOY TO THE WORLD, THE BABY'S BORN

HER NAME IS ANNA NOELLE,
BORN THIS CHRISTMAS DAY
SEVEN POUND EIGHT OUNCES SHE WEIGHS,
SHE'LL BRING JOY TO OUR WORLD,
SHE'LL BRING JOY TO OUR WORLD.

Yes, my little girl was born exactly nine months after the death of her namesake and grandma.=

Many of the friends I've made working in TV had not been on-air folks but behind-the-scenes people, primarily cameramen. That's probably because of all the time I spent riding with them in the car or news truck going to and from a story. Jack Miller and I sat across from each other through many years together at Channel 2. Most of our conversations had little to do with the story we were crafting together, instead being about what was going on in our lives. His divorce, my mother's death and the births of my children, his strained relationship with his kids and my displeasure with Channel 2 management. Of course, boys will be boys, as our rides were also filled with sophomoric humor involving farting, dick jokes and other silly topics. I generally kept the shenanigans between the two of us to the news car, but there was at least one time where he decided to share an off-color comment to an unsuspecting elderly woman.

We were in Little Italy getting ready to talk to the locals about the upcoming St. Anthony festival when a sweet-looking senior citizen came up to Jack and I and, in broken English, said, *"Antonio, God bless you, you-a much bigger man in-a-person than-you-ona TV---"*

As I smiled, Jack chimed in and said, "Look at his feet, they're size fifteen, and you know what that means. He's proportional all over."

I couldn't believe what Jack had just said. Walking away, the grandma's face turned as red as a ripe roma tomato. I told Jack he had better watch what he says in Little Italy. "You may have offended that woman, and she's going to go back and tell her son Guido, who, in turn, will have one of his boys in *la famiglia* order you a pair of custom cement shoes. You'll be wearing them as you go floating down the Patapsco River, swimming with the fishes."

Mafiosi stereotypes aside, the folks of Little Italy were proud to see one of their own on TV. *Tony's Travels* made lots of stops at their fundraisers and events. It was an annual tradition where I would roll up my sleeves and join the ladies in the basement of St. Leo's church as we made thousands of ravioli's and belted out *"That's amore"* to the camera. The old timers enjoyed kidding me because I spoke very little Italian.

I told them, "The only Italian words I know are the ones you can't say on the television."

One day while I was doing a live introduction from the streets of Little Italy and I said, "This is Tony Pagnotti," an old paisano walked up to me and says, "Hey, Antonio, why you missapronounce you name? What's this pag-not-ee. In Italian you-say pan-yott-ee." He proceeded to tell me *pagnotti* translated to small loaves of bread.

Even though I continued to use the Anglicized version of Pagnotti when saying my name, the *Baltimore Sons of Italy* honored me in 1993 by naming me its *Man of the Year* .

I was truly humbled to be selected for the yearly award. Past recipients included Baltimore magazine owner Steve Geppi. Born in Little Italy, Steve's life is truly a rags to riches story. As a former letter carrier right out of high school he would often ask folks along his route if they had any old comics in the basement from their kids' collection they would like to get rid of. Sifting through the donations he would find valuable collectible editions worth big bucks. That entrepreneurial spirit along with wise investments launched his own comic distributorship business. Today Diamond Comics International is the largest company of its kind in the world, When I did a Tony's Travels feature story on Steve's success I called him the Baltimore boy who went "From Mailman to Millionaire""

At the Awards Ceremony there was a big banquet with plenty of pasta, prosciutto and various old world delicacies were on the menu. A live band, Little Italy's own legendary Monaldi Brothers had us all dancing the tarantella. Former Baltimore Mayor Tommy D'Alessandro was on-hand to congratulate me and present a plaque from his sister, Senator Nancy Pelosi, who is now Speaker of the House. I was so moved by the evening and the tribute bestowed upon me. In expressing my thanks, I told the gathering, with a tear in my eye, "Oh, how I wish my mother could have been here tonight. I know she's smiling down on us all because for her it doesn't get any better than this, a roomful of paisanos, eating Italian food, dancing to Italian songs, and all of them celebrating and saying great things about her baby boy, Anthony."

One of the best perks of being on TV is that you not only get the best tickets to shows, events and games in town, but you get in to them all for free. It's a classic case of the media and promotional departments using each other for their own purposes. Even though there are no guarantees of coverage, event folks know if they throw freebies at the TV folks, we are, in return, more inclined to give their show or even a spot on the news. Beyond free admissions, often times the promoter is willing to arrange something special for anchors and reporters. Every time Sesame Street, the circus or another family event came to town, Edie Brown, the longtime PR lady of the Baltimore Arena, would allow me to take Alee and Annie backstage for photo opportunities with the stars of the show. They'd be also given free promotional merchandise. Being the shrewd media-savvy public relations person that she was, Edie would ensure coverage of the event by getting me personally involved in some sort of shtick.

When the *Greatest Show on Earth* came to town, you can bet I was riding an elephant or dressing up to be a clown. It's a win-win situation: I would get a great TV story out of it and the circus would be happy with the grande dame of media relations for getting them free publicity.

One of my favorite annual promotional stunts was sponsored by the Phillips Crab Restaurants. Every year prior to the running of the Preakness Stakes in Baltimore, Philips would stage the media crab race at Lexington Market. About a dozen participants from TV, radio and newspaper would be given a live crab to race at center court. At stake was a catered crab feast for all the employees at the winner's media outlet. As a crab jockey, you would get on your knees behind the crawling crustacean in an attempt to coax him across the finish line. The only rule is that you couldn't touch the crab.

But, one year, in the heat of the action and with my crab losing steam in second place, I slightly pushed the hard shell and sent it whizzing across the finish line. However, the referee didn't see the infraction and raised my hand in victory. With a scene right out of pro wrestling, the crowd went crazy, yelling at the official that I should have been disqualified for breaking the rules of the contest. Of course, all the mayhem made for a great *Tony's Travels*. In addition to the crab feast I would be getting for my colleagues, the Phillips folks handed me a gold-plated, anatomically-correct, crab-shaped trophy. For a second or two I thought about stepping forward and saying I couldn't accept the win in good conscience. But then I changed my mind, since all is fair in love, war and crab races.

23

WELCOMING AN ITALIAN BOSS TO THE TV 2 FAMILY

After nearly a year without a permanent General Manager at the helm, a station-wide corporate memo announced in 1998 that WMAR's man at the top would be Vic Lazatti . My first thought was that he couldn't be any worse than the departed Jim Barnes. My second thought was that having a fellow goombah in charge might improve my fortunes at TV 2, in more ways than one. Things between us got off to a great start. We were both on the same page when it came to the importance of a TV station's connection to the audience that it serves. I introduced him to many of the community leaders with whom I had developed relationships over the years. I talked to him about my desire for the station to broadcast a weekly local children's talent show that I would host.

After seeing the rapport I had with our viewers, he said he wanted to run promo spots on our air that would bill me as Baltimore's "TV Goodwill Ambassador." Our promotion department put together a few thirty-second spots, showing me having fun out on the town, visiting sick children in the hospital and interviewing characters who were a part of *Tony's Travels*. Accompanying the inspirational video was an original song that said, *"You can call him Tony, or even Pag will do, but he'll always be your friend on Channel 2."*

I was flattered with my newfound promotion and praise, but would I be in line for a raise? I broached the subject with Vic, making sure to also provide him with the details of the fifty percent pay cut I took from the previous administration. He sympathized with what I went through, but told me that he would have to abide by the mandatory, companywide, standard two-year contract that stipulated yearly raises to employees could not exceed two percent. Not exactly the kind of pay boost that would have me rolling in the dough. But, looking on the bright side, I could say my pay cut was now forty-eight percent. More importantly, I figured signing the agreement would give me two years of job security, considering a new news director had not yet been named.

In my thirty years in TV, I think I've worked for twenty news directors. I say think because I've probably forgotten a few along the way who didn't hold the job long enough for them to make an impression. While we on-air talent certainly lead nomadic lives, news directors are also a peripatetic bunch.

Once in a while, they leave on their own accord, but, most often, when things aren't going right for one reason or another at a station, it's the news director who gets the boot. There is an old saying in TV: the day a news director is hired, he is also fired. It's just that the timetable hasn't been worked out yet.

Rumor central around the station was that the leading candidate for news director was a guy named Curt Jones, who had held similar posts in such large markets as Boston and Philadelphia. Sure enough, the buzz about Jones turned out to be true when a memo came out, officially announcing his appointment. One week later, the staff gathered in the conference room where we would meet our new leader. In walked a sharply dressed man in his 40's with a warm smile. He put us all at ease by saying that he was privileged to be working with such a group of talented people. And he had no plans to make major personnel changes. He went on to say how he would be meeting with us individually to get our input and suggestions on what he could do to lead us back to the top of the ratings heap. He ended his pep talk by saying, "I will be asking you for some other very important suggestions, such as, where can you get the best steamed crabs?" And with that, he let out a hearty laugh and we headed back to the newsroom with a feeling that we would be under the charges of a likeable, fair and competent leader. Within a few weeks our initial assessment seemed to lift the sagging newsroom morale.

About a month later, I was walking through the station lobby when I ran into our station's former promotions director, who had left five years prior to take a job elsewhere..

Melissa said she was in Baltimore for a day and wanted to visit her former colleagues. When she told me the station she was presently working for, I said, "Oh, that's where our new news director Curt Jones came from."

The mention of his name brought a scowl to Melissa's face. "Oh, you mean Curt Jones, the anti-Christ?"

I said, "You have to be kidding, we can't be taking about the same guy."

Explaining she had to run, Melissa waved good bye and said, "Just wait, and you'll see what I'm talking about."

Sure enough, it only took a month or so before many in the newsroom witnessed the transformation. Apparently, his modus operandi at previous stations was the same. He initially comes to a station and kills the staff with praise and compliments. Then, after a short period of time, he announces that, in order to take the station to the top, he must make some changes.

Within a few days, a longtime anchor and two reporters were sent packing. In addition, Jones said that in order to meet a stringent corporate budget edict, an immediate freeze was being put on overtime and all salary increases. He concluded that any of us who had any problems with the new policies should consider looking for another job. Morale sunk to an all-time low at 6400 York Road. Just when I thought I had escaped the wrath Curt came marching up to me and said that, before I left for the day, I needed to go upstairs and talk to Lazatti.

When I walked into his office, I knew I wasn't being called in to be invited to his house for dinner. With a stern look, he began, "I don't want you to think of this as a demotion, but, in response to a mandate from corporate to trim our staff and budget, you are going to become a part-time employee, and take on an exciting new role that, in the long run, might have you earning a good deal of money. You will be coming out of the news department and, in a way, you will become a freelance host for a new show we will be doing with Home Depot."

No matter how he tried to spin my new role, the bottom line was that I would only be guaranteed twenty hours of work a week. Also, I would lose my health benefits, since I would now be a part-time employee. On top of that, I would no longer be doing feature stories or weather. He explained that, since I would no longer be a member of the news department, I could appear on commercially-sponsored local programs in which I would be paid talent fees directly by the sponsoring company. I asked him how we could just suddenly stop doing the type of good news stories that I had become well known for with the viewers in Baltimore.

With his best attempt to look compassionate, Vic replied, "Research shows people want less of the light-hearted features and more of the *live, local, and late-breaking* news each night."

Sitting there, I had the same feeling I did when I sat in the very same office a few years earlier, the day I told his predecessor he was sticking a knife through my heart. But this time around, I chose not to try and convince the General Manager to reconsider his decision. I realized that I had become a white elephant in the world of *"live, local, late-breaking"* TV news. My type of "good news" creature was quickly becoming extinct. I felt a sense of rejection and depression but managed to smile. The silver lining to all of these stormy clouds was that, as a non-news employee, I would no longer be subjected to the wrath of "Hurricane Curt."

When Vic told me I was exiting the newsroom, I didn't realize that also meant vacating the premises. I was informed that, since I would no longer be doing my stories, I should pack my belongings from my desk and relocate downstairs to the programming department. My new spot was a dusty little cubicle that was situated at the end of a darkened hall next to a fire exit door. Not exactly the type of digs you'd expect for the host of a new home improvement show.

24

LEARNING NEW TOOLS
OF THE TRADE (2001)

The concept for the half-hour program was born from how most local shows in TV originate: when there is a sponsor willing to fund it. The TV 2 sales department got a commitment from Home Depot to run a half-hour program, which would feature members of its staff demonstrating do-it-yourself projects. As host, I would play the role of the inquisitive, unskilled homeowner who would observe the experts. It was a role I could personally identify with, as I've never been able to so much as hammer a nail. I didn't hide the fact that I was an unhandy guy around my own house. On the show I would often tell viewers, "My wife is the one who wears the tool belt in our family." Sandy was also the major breadwinner in the family, now that I was a part time employee with no health benefits.

If there was one benefit to my demotion, it was that the new gig was easy. Once a week, all I had to do was show up at The Home Depot store where we would be taping the half-hour segment to air Saturday morning on TV 2. Videographer/producer Mel Murphy would have our demo experts and their projects lined up for the shoot. Before taping began, I would familiarize myself with the show rundown and make a few notes of things I would say. There was no written script. It was primarily me ad-libing and interacting with my "Homers," as they were called, for an informative and entertaining half hour of TV. When the taping was finished, so was my work for the week. Although I was being paid for twenty hours weekly, I was working one to two hours.

When I asked Lazatti if the programming department could use me for hosting any other shows or doing commercials, he said, "Not right now, but maybe down the road."

As I left his office, I thought, *I'm headed down a dead-end road.*

Despite the easy money I was earning, I had grown increasingly unhappy, restless and bored with my professional lot in life. I would often find myself sitting at my cramped desk, with a lot of free time to brood over what my career had become. The one bright spot was my other part-time job as an adjunct speech instructor at the Community College of Baltimore County. I would teach two to three sections of Speech 101. My students were adults going back to get a degree, foreign students, and teenagers fresh out of high school. As an adjunct you get paid very little, but the rewards come in being able to instill confidence in your students and watching them become better in their communication skills. The satisfaction and stability that a full-time teaching career could provide was something I could no longer find in TV. However, I found that, despite my years of experience as a professional communicator, CCBC and other area colleges told me that a minimum of a Master's degree would be needed for me to be considered for a full-time instructor position. But, at the time, I had neither the motivation nor the financial resources to consider going for an advanced degree.

During its first year, *Around the House* became popular with viewers, which prompted Home Depot to sponsor the program for an additional two years. As part of a promotional campaign, life-size cutouts of yours truly wearing a big tool belt were placed at the entrance of Home Depot stores in the area. If only viewers knew that their tool-toting host thought that a screwdriver was a drink and a jigsaw was a puzzle. Even though no one at the station kept tabs on how few hours I was putting in each week, I felt the need for a more productive twenty-hour week. When I told that to the TV program director, he said he could use me in on-location car commercials, in which the dealerships would also pay me a talent fee for my services. Those appearances were few and far between, but it gave me a sense of purpose, not to mention a little something extra in my paycheck. With such a flexible part-time job, I started a media training business called Public Performance. From my years of doing interviews with public officials and business executives, I noticed how many of them could benefit from the services of a communications coach to prepare them for TV appearances. After contacting a number of firms and organizations to let them know about the services I provided, I started getting training jobs.

I would go to a company's offices and work directly with a C.E.O on his telegenic skills, and then we would do some role-playing. I would pose as the TV interviewer while my friend and photographer Jack Miller would tape the segment. After each take, I would play it back for the interviewee for critique and analysis. I enjoyed seeing the progress that was made at the end of a day-long training session. Someday, I thought I could turn Public Performance into a full-time career, but, for now, the only guaranteed income I could count on was from the part-time TV home improvement show, to which I felt nailed.

The bottom line was that I sorely missed doing the feel-good stories that made me feel good. I no longer could shine the spotlight on the colorful characters, the caring and compassionate everyday people, or the vibrant neighborhoods that were my TV world. It was difficult when longtime viewers would come up to me in the street or in stores and say, "Hey, how come we don't see you on the news anymore? We looked forward to seeing your stories. They made us smile."

While I was tempted to answer, "research shows more people prefer bad news to good news," I would usually half-heartedly reply, "What do you think of my *Around the House* show?" Truth be told, my heart was no longer in my job. For the first time in my life, what I did was simply a job, a means to the end of collecting a check. It was a livelihood, not a lifelong passion.

I was looking forward to having my feel-good juices rejuvenated in a few months, when I would, once again, be the host for the MDA Jerry Lewis Labor Day Telethon. It was the annual labor of love and a family reunion for me. I would share the spotlight with many of Jerry's Kids and their families, whose inspirational stories I had told over the years on Channel 2. But just when I thought that things couldn't get any worse for me, I received a phone call from an MDA mom whom I had known, along with her teenage son, for many years. She asked if I heard a rumor going around that Channel 2 would no longer be broadcasting the telethon. I told her that couldn't be true, since WMAR was one of the first stations in the country to air the MDA telethon, beginning back in the 60s. Later that day, I was passing Vic in the hall and said, "You know, I got a call from an MDA mom who said she heard we weren't going to be carrying the telethon."

As he kept walking, he replied, "Oh... why don't you stop by my office before you leave today?"

Incredibly, later that day I was told the rumor was indeed true. The GM said that, as much as he would have loved to keep the telethon on TV 2, he said with declining revenue the station could no longer afford to continue broadcasting the twenty-four-hour fundraising event. I spent the next several weeks trying to explain to the MDA families, who I had spent my last fifteen Labor Day weekends with, that the annual show would go on, but, regrettably, not on Channel 2, and without me. Fortunately, within a few weeks, local UHF outlet Channel 54 agreed to become the new telethon station in Baltimore. I knew I had to get off the sinking ship that was WMAR but realized I couldn't wait for someone to throw me a lifejacket. There were still stations out there that I felt would welcome a veteran, high-profile, good-news personality to their staff. Such a nationwide search would be best conducted by a powerful agent. The words of Carol Cooper echoed in my mind when I had decided to sever ties with her: "Don't try to come running back to me."

Even though I hadn't talked to her since that conversation, I swallowed my pride and called her office. I explained my circumstances and asked if she would take me back as a client. True to her word, Carol said she would not and wished me well. Of course, there were other agents out there that I could have pursued, but deep down I questioned whether I had the motivation to start all over again in a new city, just to build up what I had already achieved in Baltimore. I kept going through the motions each week, taping *Around the House*, rationalizing that I shouldn't look a gift horse in the mouth.

But, one day, I felt like someone had kicked me in the teeth when it was announced Vic Lazzati was leaving the station and his successor was already in the building. , Curt Jones was promoted to WMAR's new GM. Talk about the second coming of the Anti- Christ. The scuttlebutt going around 6400 York Rd was that, Jones was being considered for GM positions at other stations. When corporate honchos got wind of this, they agreed if he were passed over at the vacancy at TV 2 he would he would be scooped up as a General Manager elsewhere. I'm sure among the main factors in making their decision, if Jones left the company, it would leave the media conglomerate without a strong minority presence in high-level management positions.

Much to my surprise, in his new role as general manager, Curt had little impact on this old part-timer. Passing me in the hall one day, he said with a smile I had learned not to trust, "Hey, Pag, *Around the House* is looking great, keep up the good work." I reasoned that maybe, in his new powerful position, it wasn't worth his effort to mess with a popular program that was making money for the station. So, weeks, months and another year went by, as my TV life consisted of hosting *Around the House* and doing occasional live, on-location commercials for car dealerships.

But, just as in life, nothing lasts forever in TV. I started to speculate that change was in the offing during our weekly tapings of *Around the House*. We usually recorded spots in advance to promote segments for the following month. So, when I noticed we weren't taping them anymore, I asked my producer, photographer and longtime Channel 2 colleague, "Why not?"

He, at first, had a look on his face that said, "Uh-oh" and then downplayed it by saying, "No reason, just switching up the format a bit." I knew something was up and that there was a move to take me down and off the show. When I cornered him and asked him what he knew, he gave a very unconvincing one-word response: "Nothing." Later that week, my suspicions were confirmed. I got a call at home from Jones and I knew he wasn't inviting me over to his house for a barbeque. He began by saying that the show was going on, but without me. Home Depot staffers would take turns hosting the weekly program. He said that, effective immediately, my part-time position was being eliminated and that, under AFTRA union contract, I would be receiving a severance payment for thirty-four weeks of wages, two weeks of compensation for each of the seventeen years

I had been employed at WMAR. He concluded by saying there were papers for me to sign before I would receive my final payout in the mail.

My first reaction was to ask him why I was being unceremoniously kicked out the door after giving blood, sweat and tears to a TV station for so many years. But I decided not to, and instead broke the cardinal rule of what a terminated employee should never do: burn bridges. With kerosene-bated breath, I lit him up by exclaiming, "Curt, I have worked with a lot of TV managers in my time, but you are the one I least respect. In a matter of just a few years, you came in to Channel 2, took a highly-rated news station and drove it in the ground."

When I paused to see if he was still on the line after that rant, he replied, "Hey, go ahead, bad mouth me all you want if that helps you get out your own bitterness and unhappiness with your career. This could be the best thing that has ever happened to you in deciding where you want to go from here."

My parting words were: "Have a Good Life." Click. Yeah, I not only burned the Jones Bridge, I blew up the river that ran beneath it.

25

IS THERE LIFE AFTER TV 2?

I was out of a TV job. I would have to file for unemployment benefits, something I hadn't done since my New Haven days. But, since then, technology had changed, which meant I could file my claim online and not have to go stand in the unemployment office line and hear, "Hey, Tony Pagnotti, are you here doing a story about us people who are out of work?"

For one of the very few times in my adult life, I was a man without a TV station. It didn't take long for viewers to notice either. A day wouldn't go by without someone coming up to me and saying, "Hey, how come you're not on TV anymore? We miss you." I would always thank them for noticing and think, *Yeah, how come I'm not on TV anymore?* Every now and then I would make a fill-in weather appearance on Fox 45, when someone was either on vacation or had called in sick. Just to get my TV fix, I would occasionally travel an hour and half up I-83 in Harrisburg to do vacation relief work at WHP-TV.

I also decided this would be a good time to finally pursue a Master's degree in Communications, so I enrolled at the College of Notre Dame Maryland for the fall semester of 2007. Having so much free time on my hands that summer, my daughters Alee and Annie pleaded with me to audition for the play *Annie*, which was being presented by a local theater group, The Glyndon Area Players. I always loved to sing and act but had never been under the stage lights. So, for the audition I belted out my rendition of Dean Martin's *That's Amore* and read from the *Annie* Script with one of the girls who was also auditioning for the show.

The next day I got a call from the show's director saying he wanted to offer me the part of Daddy Warbucks. When I told my girls I got the role of Warbucks, they were jumping up and down. What I didn't realize when I accepted that the role was that it was a major one, with lots of dialogue and five solo numbers. The director also asked if I would shave my head *a la* Warbucks. but I declined, saying that being bald would not be a good look for a freelance weatherman looking for employment opportunities. So, for each of the eight performances, I had to wear a skull cap which had to be meticulously glued around the top of my forehead and hairline. Despite all the rehearsals and hard work, I thoroughly enjoyed my stage debut. It was such a different experience from TV, where it's just talking to a camera. In theater, your audience is in front of you, providing instant feedback with their applause and laughter.

Following my last performance, I realized the first week

of September would also bring another first-time experience to my life – Graduate school. But as fate would have it, I got a phone call from the chief meteorologist at Sinclair Broadcasting – a Baltimore-based broadcasting company which owns ninety TV stations around the country, including Fox 45. Vytas Reid said there was a full-time weathercaster position opening at the company's corporate facility in Cockeysville and asked if I would be interested in coming in for an interview. The next day I interviewed for the job, which involved doing daily weathercasts for Sinclair's affiliated stations in cities such as Pittsburgh, Greensboro, St Louis, Birmingham, and Las Vegas.

No, the position did not require a lot of traveling, either. In a very shrewd and cost-effective way, the weather reports all originated from the Sinclair studios in Cockeysville and were beamed to the various local affiliates around the country. Five staff weathercasters would each provide forecasts for three different Sinclair cities each night. So, instead of having to hire fifteen meteorologists in the cities of the affiliated stations, Sinclair was able to get the work done with workhouse weathercasters in the corporate studio. I was impressed with the efficiency and advancements in broadcast technology which enabled such an operation. The day after the interview, I got a call from Vytas offering me the full-time position with full benefits and a two-year contract. I was back to broadcasting. Grad school would have to be put on the back-burner.

But Sinclair had gotten some heat from industry watchdogs for its innovative weather syndication concept. The critics claimed that, when an anchorman at the Sinclair station in Tallahassee would say, "Let's check in with Tony

Pagnotti to see if we'll need our umbrellas tomorrow," viewers had no idea that I was not in Florida but in a Baltimore studio, 1,000 miles away. You couldn't help but believe that the weathercaster was local since we used maps with the regional towns, satellites and radar maps. Why, I'd even plug in some local flavor by telling folks it was going to be a great day for the big barbecue festival going on in town this weekend.

The critics charged Sinclair with making the public into believing the forecaster was in the studio of the local station. The company response was that the anchor people never introduced the weather segment by saying, "Tony is here with us now." However, I must say most viewers thought the weathercaster was in their community. I received more than a few emails from people I knew from my travels around the country that would say, "Hey, it was great seeing you on TV last night doing the weather. I've been living in Greensboro for the past five years, what part of town are you in? We should get together." I'd email them back explaining that, through the magic of TV technology, I was on the airwaves in their town every night, but was hundreds of miles away in Maryland.

It was fun being back on TV, but I didn't feel like I really was, as my broadcasts were not seen on the local Sinclair station. So, whenever people would see me at the store or in the street, they would ask, "What are you doing now, since we don't see you on TV anymore?" But the bottom line was that I had a secure, full-time, on-air position, at least for the time being.

In the here-we-go-again department, about two years into my employment at Sinclair, a bombshell was dropped. Corporate officials said they would cease doing news altogether at most of its affiliated stations. That meant, of course, there would be no need any longer for eight weathercasters to be kept on staff. News manager Joe Defeo called me into his office and explained that the weather staff would be disbanded, with the exception of one position. He said that three of the stations needed a weatherman to provide morning cut-ins for either the *Today Show* or *Good Morning America*. He wanted to know if I would be interested in the position. He thought my personality would be well-suited for the assignment.

I said, "Yes," in a heartbeat. I thanked God for allowing me to barely escape another termination bullet. My fellow weathercasters, who had all been given two-week pink slips, seemed a bit jealous and envious that the guy with the least seniority survived the execution. I felt their pain, but, quite frankly, it was overshadowed by my own pleasure.

I rang in 2006 with a very early start to the New Year. In my new role, I had to be into work by 4:30 AM to prepare my morning cut-ins for Greensboro, Tallahassee and St Louis. While all the other weather studios in the building were shut down, my little weather world was a tiny room with a desk for my computer and a green screen wall where I would stand to deliver my reports. Corporate honchos did not want to staff the early bird shift with an engineer. So, on the first floor of this ten-story building, every early morning, it was me, myself and I. The camera I would stand in front of was preset for my height and background computer graphics. Between the hours of six and nine I would jump in front of the green screen and crank out thirty-second and one-minute updates for my three stations. No sooner did I finish St Louis than it would be time to flip my maps and towns and move on to Tallahassee, with Greensboro waiting in the wings.

Yes, there were times during the fast-paced commotion that I would forget what state I was in, but, fortunately, each segment was digitally recorded so I could redo any mess ups. Once I finished an update, I would press a button on an electronic box called the *telestreamer*. I would find the appropriate station destination and send my video clip into cyber space. Within a few minutes, engineers in control rooms hundreds of miles away would snag my weather update and get it on their air in seconds. If, thirty years earlier when I first got into the business, you told me that someday I would be all by myself in a tiny room in the wee hours of the morning, digitally recording and transmitting weather updates for stations around the country, I would say you were crazy. But I enjoyed the autonomy of my job. There were no management folks to answer to because my day was done around 9 AM, just about when everyone else was coming to work. There were many days, though, when I felt like the Maytag repair man, the loneliest guy in town.

New Year's Day, 2007, began tragically for me. My father, Tony, who had been incapacitated from an unexpected stroke nearly two years earlier, died. As much as I grieved his death, I was relieved his suffering was over. He was always the healthy workhouse, never missing a day in the pharmacy. And right up to the day he suffered the stroke at eighty-seven, he had been walking five miles a day around his neighborhood. The stroke left him partially paralyzed in a Veterans Hospital in Scranton. In the end, he didn't know who he was. But the man certainly left his mark on all those he touched while running Pagnotti's Pharmacy. In delivering his eulogy, I commented on how honored I felt to hear generations of families at his funeral talk about the impact he had on their lives.

Driving home to Baltimore after the service, I got to thinking about how his dream was for me to follow in his footsteps and take over the pharmacy. As much as I realized I had neither the aptitude nor the passion to do so, I heard his words echoing from what he often told me as a young man, "You know, if you become a pharmacist and take over the business, you will be your own boss, and you'll never have to worry about working for bosses who can control and dictate your destiny." As the old Mark Twain quote goes, "The older I got, I was amazed at how much wiser my father had become."

Despite the popularity of the syndicated morning weather cut-ins during its two year run, corporate decided to pull the plug on my gig, citing financial considerations. I can't imagine that my modest salary was breaking the corporate bank, or that my studio lights were running up Sinclair's electric bill. But I was done second-guessing TV's decision makers. With a lot of free time on my hands once again, I felt it would be an ideal time for me to volunteer somewhere in the community, where my communication skills could be put to good use. I heard that *Catholic Charities of Baltimore* operated a center called Christopher Place Employment Academy. The residential learning facility was a comprehensive training center for formerly homeless and incarcerated men who were looking for a second chance in getting their lives back on track. It sounded like a program in which I would love to be a part. I contacted the director of the academy and asked if I could be of service in any way. He said they were looking for someone who could teach the men how to effectively communicate in a job interview.

"Look no further," I said. I developed a role-playing workshop called "Confidence in Communication" and began teaching it on a weekly basis. My students have been a true inspiration for me in their commitment to turning their lives around. I don't receive a paycheck, but it is the most rewarding job I have ever had. My experience at the Academy in being able to make an impact on my students' lives was the deciding factor for me to take the steps necessary to pursue a career as a full-time communications teacher.

So, toward that end, in September of 2008, there I was, a graduate student of Contemporary Communications at the College of Notre Dame. Was it crazy for someone who was approaching his senior years to go back to college for an advanced degree? Looking around the classroom, most of my fellow students were female and in their twenties. Sure, I was feeling a bit like a fish out of water, but, after class, one young lady, Michelle Eurice, sure helped me put my new college experience in perspective. She said that she had told her mother that there was this older guy named Tony Pagnotti that she met in class.

Her mom replied, "You tell Mr. Pagnotti that, when you were a pre-mee in the neo-natal Intensive Care Unit at

Johns Hopkins, he held you as he was broadcasting for the Miracle Network Telethon."

Michelle and I had a good laugh. I was feeling old, but in a good way. Technology sure has changed since my college days. Back in the day, you needed chalk for the blackboard. Now, you go to Blackboard on your computer and have online group discussions with your classmates and professor. And when you finish that twenty-page research paper, no need to bring the document to class with you. You can get it to your professor electronically by placing it in his Digital Dropbox. So, who says you can't teach an old dog new tricks?

It is now September 2010 and I am entering my final semester of grad school My final thesis project, *"TV NEWSMAN-MY SCRIPTED AND UNSCRIPTED LIFE "* is what you have been reading for the past 200-some pages. From a scholarly perspective, I hope you have found it to be educational, insightful and entertaining. For me, it has been both therapeutic and thought-provoking, being able to relive the twists and turns of my personal and professional life. It has been quite the roller coaster, but the ride, with all its ups and down, has been oh, so thrilling.

AND, FINALLY, TONIGHT, ON WPAG TV NEWS...

TONY ON CAM CU

You know, my uncle had to die for me to break into broadcasting. It was the summer of 1971 and I was home in Scranton after completing my freshman year at Susquehanna University. During my freshman year there, I felt I had found my calling. My passion was being a disc jockey known as *Big Daddy Pags* on the campus station. So, with rock-and-roll demonstration tape in hand, I called on the three radio stations in Downtown Scranton. I was rejected by all three stations for any summertime fill-in work. They all said I wasn't quite ready yet for the Scranton airwaves. I was dejected and depressed, thinking that Scranton wasn't exactly the broadcasting mecca of America and that I would be working in the family pharmacy the rest of the summer.

Later that week, there was sad news in our family: my mother's brother Nick, a prominent member of the business community had passed away. His wife called and asked if I would deliver the eulogy for my Uncle Nick, since I had a close relationship with him. I told her it would be my pleasure and delivered heartfelt words at his service. The next day, my Aunt called me and said that the General Manager of Scranton station WICK was at the funeral service and asked her who the young man was that delivered such a wonderful eulogy. She told Mr. Dobbs that it was Nick's nephew, Tony, who was at his station recently looking for a radio job. He told her to have me come in and talk to his program director immediately. So, when I arrived at WICK the next day, the program director said they had a fill-in on-air summer slot from 2-6 PM they'd like to offer me. I wouldn't be playing music though. Their format was all talk. Listeners could call in and discuss everything from politics and life to their favorite movies and TV shows. I couldn't sleep the night before. I tossed and turned, thinking about how my uncle's death resulted in my baptism into the business of broadcasting.

THANKS FOR JOINING US AT WPAG-TV
HOPE TO SEE YOU AGAIN TOMORROW

EPILOGUE • MAY 2010

I sometimes wonder how, if it weren't for my uncle's death in 1972, I might not have wound up in front of a TV camera. Instead I would have found myself behind the counter at Pagnotti's Pharmacy, filling prescriptions and fulfilling my father's dream. I have often felt that what drove me to pursue a career in the high-profile, risky business of television, which screams look-at-me, was a desire to gain my father's approval and acceptance. During the final weeks of his life, my dad's once razor-sharp mind was being taken over by dementia. When my wife, daughters and I would stop by, he often would not recognize us. In one of my last visits before his death, I was holding his hand as he stared blankly into my eyes. When a nurse walked in, she decided to test his state of awareness.

"Hey, who is that young man holding your hand?"

With a smile, nod and a squeeze of my hand, he softly replied, "That's my son, Tony Pagnotti. He's on Television."

As I put the finishing touches on this book, I look down and see a ring on one of my typing fingers. Around the gold setting of the ruby-stone graduation ring, the lettering reads, *Temple University School of Pharmacy 1949*. By the time you read this, I should have another ring on my finger that reads *College of Notre Dame of Maryland, MA, Contemporary*

Communications, 2010. Hopefully, by then I will also be a full-time college instructor. I can't wait for that day, when someone stops me on the street and says, "Aren't you that guy who used to be on TV?"

To which I'll reply, "Yeah, but now you can just call me professor."

TEN YEARS LATER
POSTSCRIPT • MAY 2020

Boy, a decade can sure fly by when you're having fun. Within months after receiving my Master's degree, I landed a great full-time job as a Communications instructor at the University of Maryland, College Park.

I loved every minute of it. I was able to teach very bright students that, no matter whether they wanted to be doctors, engineers or entrepreneurs, outstanding communication skills are essential in order to make it to the top in any given field. In 2018, I decided that it was time to retire from my full-time position and instead work part-time as an adjunct professor at two area community colleges.

Up until last year, I was also the weekend morning weathercaster on FOX 45 Baltimore. During my last broadcast, they surprised me with a very nice tribute video congratulating me on my retirement and 40-year broadcasting career.

After four decades, I do miss being on TV but realize that most of the folks I see on-camera these days are young enough to be my children. Being a 67-year-old Social Security recipient and proud grandpa now, I realize my TV days are probably behind me. But being able to reminisce over 40 years of cherished memoires whenever I want will keep me going until the day I'm ready to:

FADE TO BLACK.

ABOUT THE AUTHOR

A native of Scranton, PA., Tony Pagnotti majored in Broadcast Journalism at Boston University. At the age of 22, he began his TV career in Asheville, N.C.

In the following years, Pagnotti worked as a reporter, anchor, and weathercaster at stations in Ohio, Connecticut, and New York.

In 1985, he was hired at WMAR-TV Baltimore, where for many years he was a well-known personality in the community. Pagnotti co–anchored the weekend Morning News on Fox 45 along with teaching communications at the University of Maryland.

Pagnotti now resides in Columbia, Maryland, and is the proud grandfather of Luke and Hazel.

Apprentice
House Press
Loyola University Maryland

Apprentice House is the country's only campus-based, student-staffed book publishing company. Directed by professors and industry professionals, it is a nonprofit activity of the Communication Department at Loyola University Maryland.

Using state-of-the-art technology and an experiential learning model of education, Apprentice House publishes books in untraditional ways. This dual responsibility as publishers and educators creates an unprecedented collaborative environment among faculty and students, while teaching tomorrow's editors, designers, and marketers.

Outside of class, progress on book projects is carried forth by the AH Book Publishing Club, a co-curricular campus organization supported by Loyola University Maryland's Office of Student Activities.

Eclectic and provocative, Apprentice House titles intend to entertain as well as spark dialogue on a variety of topics. Financial contributions to sustain the press's work are welcomed. Contributions are tax deductible to the fullest extent allowed by the IRS.

To learn more about Apprentice House books or to obtain submission guidelines, please visit www.apprenticehouse.com.

Apprentice House
Communication Department
Loyola University Maryland
4501 N. Charles Street
Baltimore, MD 21210
Ph: 410-617-5265
info@apprenticehouse.com • www.apprenticehouse.com

CPSIA information can be obtained
at www.ICGtesting.com
Printed in the USA
LVHW081809140421
684383LV00039B/1688

9 781627 203425